THE ADMINISTRATION OF JUSTICE

IN IRELAND

V.T.H. DELANY

EDITED BY CHARLES LYSAGHT

Institute of Public Administration
Dublin

© Institute of Public Administration 1962, 1965, 1970, 1975
ISBN 0 902173 64 2

First Edition 1962
Second Edition 1965, revised by Vincent Grogan
Third Edition 1970, revised by Vincent Grogan
Fourth Edition 1975, revised by Charles Lysaght
Reprinted 1978
Reprinted 1979
Reprinted 1980
Made and printed in the Republic of Ireland
by Task Print (Dublin) Ltd.

Reprinted 1980
Made and printed in the Republic of Ireland
by Task Print (Dublin) Ltd.

CONTENTS

Preface   vi

Chapter 1   The Nature and Sources of Irish Law   1

Chapter 2   The Background of the Irish Judicial System   13

Chapter 3   The System of Courts in Ireland 1800-1921   19

Chapter 4   The Constitutional Changes 1921-1924   32

Chapter 5   The Courts Since 1922   38

Chapter 6   The Criminal Jurisdiction of the Courts   43

Chapter 7   The Civil Jurisdiction of the Courts   57

Chapter 8   The Personnel of the Courts   72

Chapter 9   The Legal Profession   84

Chapter 10   The Finances of the Law   93

Further Reading   100

Index   102

PREFACE

It gives me much pleasure to have the opportunity of bringing up to date the late Professor Vincent Delany's work. Since the last revision of the book, carried out by Vincent Grogan in 1970, the major developments worthy of note have been the Courts Act 1971 and the Prosecution of Offences Act 1974. I have expanded and updated the parts of the book describing the jurisdiction of the various Courts and also made reference to the Court of Justice of the European Communities and the organs of the European Convention on Human Rights; in addition, the functions of the newly created Director of Public Prosecutions are outlined. The section on legal aid has been rewritten to take account of recent developments. I have incorporated references to the views expressed in the valuable reports of the Committee on Court Practice and Procedure. I have not materially changed the original text otherwise; in particular, I have not sought to interpose my own opinions with Professor Delany's, almost all of which retain their relevance in a legal system that has not changed greatly in the thirteen years since the book was first published.

CHARLES LYSAGHT

CHAPTER I

THE NATURE AND SOURCES OF IRISH LAW

Professor W. M. Geldart, a former holder of the Vinerian Chair of Law in the University of Oxford, once drew attention to the fact that writers commonly draw a distinction between 'law' and 'laws', and he pointed out that these two expressions indicate a difference between two separate aspects of legal science. The legal system of a country may be regarded either as a series of separate and distinct, individual rules, or it may be regarded as a coherent unity. Each individual 'law', moreover, forms part of the whole system of what we call *the* law, and in the sense in which the average layman thinks of the problem, he is inclined to regard each rule as being a fragmentary part of the whole.

This distinction, moreover, is emphasised by the fact that as a matter of experience, most legal systems may be broken down into rules which are not derived by any process of analysis from the law as a whole, but have an independent existence, and rules which have existed from time immemorial, or are said by a judiciary to have done so. Rules having an independent existence are generally found to have originated in the activity of a legislature, and are termed 'statute law', while rules which have attributed to them immemorial antiquity are, by contrast, called 'the common law.'

A little over two hundred years ago, William Blackstone wrote his treatise entitled *Commentaries on the Laws of England*, and he divided the English legal system in this way, into written or statute law and unwritten or common law; he went on to explain that the latter consisted of general customs by which the proceedings in the ordinary courts were guided and directed. The validity of these customs was decided by the judges; records of their judgments were preserved and it was the rule to be bound by them when the same point came up for decision again. Blackstone was here adverting to the essential feature of English law, that the basic principles of the law of England were originally established by the judges when they decided cases, on the theory that they were 'declaring' the ancient customary law of the kingdom, for the expression 'common law' meant the law common to the whole people of England. Nowadays, we tend to regard law as being the product of the Oireachtas, as indeed the bulk of it is; but it must not be forgotten that statute law is a comparatively late growth in the Anglo-Irish legal system, and is preceded in point of time by the collection of general customs called 'the common law.'

A further distinction must be drawn, which often leads to confusion. The term 'common law' is frequently used to describe that system of law derived from the law of England which has been extended to those countries which have at one time or another formed part of the British Empire (including the United States), in contradistinction to the systems of law operative in most of the other countries of the world which are derived from Roman law. Common law in this larger sense, of course, embraces both the written and unwritten aspects of the English system, and so includes the common law in the narrow sense of judge-made or judge-found law.

Assuming, then, that the components of the common law can be described in this way, it is possible to state that the basis of the system of law operating on the island of Ireland is to be found in the legal apparatus which the Normans brought with them to Ireland in the twelfth century, in so far as that apparatus has been expanded and added to by the activity of the courts since that time, and by the activity of the various parliaments which have claimed authority to legislate for the country as a whole. To those who object to the use of the geographical expressions 'Ireland' and 'Irish law' in this connection, it can be said that there is a much greater similarity between the law of the Republic of Ireland and that of Northern Ireland than there is between either system and that of England. The passing of eight centuries of uniform legal development has left a mark on the Irish system which the political alterations of 1921 have not yet had time to erase. Much of the divergence between the English and Irish legal systems came in the nineteenth century, before the 1921 settlement, and such differences as have been created since are due mainly to the adoption by the Parliament of Northern Ireland of many of the statutes passed for England since 1921.

Before examining the process by which the common law of England came to be imported into Ireland, it will be helpful to review in more detail the sources of that system as they exist today.

Legislation

Legislation is law enacted by a responsible parliament. In England, the earliest enacted law was made by the King with the approval of his Council, and then, as parliament became an institution acceptable to Englishmen, law was made by statute. At first, statutes did not follow any set pattern and it was commonplace for the English judiciary to query their validity or effect, but by the time of the Tudors, statutes had assumed the form which they have since retained, namely, an enactment by the Queen "with the advice and consent of" the Lords and Commons. By then the judges were accepting the validity of statute law, though as late as the time of Blackstone (in the middle of the eighteenth century), it was still being suggested that judges might disregard a statute that infringed natural or divine law. The English judges, however, eventually accepted the position that parliament was supreme, and that anything enacted by it would have to be accepted by the courts. On the other hand, they tended to regard legislation as a subordinate source of law, and to hold that the common law built up from the system of precedent was the predominant factor. As a result, they tried to construe statutes as being in conformity with the common law wherever possible. The great bulk of legislation over the last hundred years, however, has produced a more realistic attitude; and, now, it is generally recognised that legislation is the primary source of law.

With the growth in importance of enacted law, the technique of statutory interpretation has developed. The interpretation of a piece of enacted law requires not only a familiarity with the meaning of technical legal terms, but also with the whole branch of the law of which the statute forms a part; in particular, it requires a knowledge of the rules of interpretation which are themselves rules of law. Thus, there is a rule against taking into account anything said or done while the statute is passing through parliament; and there are certain statutory rules with regard to the construction to be placed on words importing number and gender. If a question as to the meaning of a statute arises in an action at law, the judge will have to decide the meaning, and his decision will be binding for all future cases in which the same question arises, just as we shall see that his decision is binding authority for future cases where a question arises as to the common law.

The legal system in the Republic of Ireland is affected by all the parliaments which formerly had authority and which now have authority within its territory. The former parliaments were (i) The Parliament of Ireland, which ended with the Act of Union 1800, and (ii) The Parliament of the United Kingdom of Great Britain and Ireland, which ended with the Irish Free State (Agreement) Act 1922. In addition, authority over the whole island of Ireland was claimed, from time to time, by the Parliament of England and by the Parliament of Great Britain (which existed from 1707 to 1800). Finally, of course (iii) the Oireachtas established by the Constitution of the Irish Free State 1922, article 12, had "sole and exclusive power for making laws for the peace, order and good government" of the Irish Free State, and it remained operative until 1937. The Parliament now having authority is the Oireachtas, or National Parliament, established under article 15 of the Constitution of Ireland 1937. One result of this is that a search for the enacted law in force involves an examination of the statutes of all these legislatures.

Judge-Made Laws

In most legal systems, the decisions of the courts given in the course of litigation are treated with a certain degree of respect, and they tend to be regarded as 'precedents' which other courts will follow at a subsequent date when called upon to decide issues of a similar nature. There are probably two reasons for this. The first is convenience, in that it is easier to be able to decide an issue by reference to an earlier determination; this phenomenon is to be found in many organisations outside the sphere of law. The second is uniformity, for if the law is not certain, then the result must be to confuse the litigant and stultify the administration of justice.

In England, this system of judicial precedent early assumed great importance. There was no authoritative text of the common law, as opposed to statute law, and it was not contained in any one book.

As we shall see later, the judicial system developed in such a way that there emerged a number of Royal Courts with a wide jurisdiction, each staffed by judges with legal experience. They were charged with administering the 'law and custom of the realm', and so, by their own efforts, they built up a considerable body of rules. These decisions of the judges tended to be uniform, and local or regional differences in the law of England disappeared. It is in their reported decisions that the common law of England is to be found and, when that system was imported into Ireland, a similar practice obtained here from the earliest times.

Although the sources of the common law are not to be found in any one authoritative text, nevertheless the common law is to be found in books; these books are called law reports and contain the reported decisions of the judges of the courts. Every case heard in one of Ireland's superior courts has an official 'record', but this merely contains the outline of the case. Some of these cases embrace points of interest to lawyers and become 'reported' cases. These reports contain the facts found by the court, the arguments put forward on either side, and the reason given by the judge for his decision. Ever since the reign of Edward I there have been lawyers in England who have been engaged in the business of reporting the decisions of the courts. The earliest of these decisions were nothing more than a series of jottings made in court, known as the Year Books, and they appeared down to the time of Henry VIII. They were followed by reports produced by lawyers under their own names. At first, these were published sporadically, and it was not until the end of the eighteenth century that reports began to be published regularly in England. In Ireland, too, the process began about that time, with the difference that there was no distinct system operating here corresponding to the Year Books or the pre-eighteenth-century reporters.

During the nineteenth century, the publishers of legal periodicals began to issue reports, and from 1866 there has been a series produced by the legal profession in England called *The Law Reports*. A similar course of events has been followed in Ireland, but neither of these semi-official systems has supplanted private enterprise. Moreover, neither *The Law Reports* nor *The Irish Reports* are 'official' in the sense that they are published under governmental authority. They are 'authorised' in the sense that the judges who have decided the cases contained in them have themselves examined and, where necessary, revised their judgments before publication; but this practice is followed by many of the private series as well.

The use of these decided cases has changed with the passage of time. As printed reports became more common, their citation in court became more frequent, and the court was expected to follow them. But the court was not *bound* to follow earlier decisions; and, at first, they were only regarded as evidence of what the law was. Gradually, however, greater weight came to be attached to them as authorities, and it can be said that, from the nineteenth century onwards in England, decided cases have been regarded as definite authority, which, in the absence of special reasons to the contrary, must be followed in the future.

This theory of 'absolutely binding' precedent meant that the decisions of a court bound all inferior tribunals. The apex of the system was the House of Lords, which held that it could not reverse itself, and all English courts which ranked below it were bound by its decisions. So also, the Court of Appeal in England was bound by itself, subject to certain exceptions. However, a decision of one High Court judge, though treated by another as of high *persuasive* authority, is not absolutely binding on him. In practice, however, he will nearly always follow it, unless he is convinced that it is wrong. On the other hand, a decision of a lower court is not binding on any court ranking above it, though, in the course of time, it may acquire an authority which even a higher court will not ignore, either because the point at issue has never been taken to a higher court, or because it has remained unquestioned for a long time. The public may have come to regard it as the law and have acted upon it, and the higher court, even though it may think the decision wrong in principle, will be reluctant to overrule it, preferring to leave this task to the legislature.

The system of absolutely binding precedents, moreover, is not as rigid as might appear at first sight. Not everything which a judge says in the course of his judgment creates a precedent, but only his statement of the law with regard to the particular facts before him. In order to find the *ratio decidendi* of the case—the principle on which it is based— it is first necessary to divorce the law stated in a judgment from the facts to which it is applied. Law reports do not follow any set form, in the sense that the judgments need not be delivered in any prescribed manner, and so the reader is free to hold his own views as to what in fact, was laid down.

It is also necessary to distinguish between the *ratio decidendi* of the case and *obiter dicta*—'things said by the way.' These are statements of law made in the course of the judgment, but not applicable to the issue between the parties to the suit. They are made by way of explanation only, and if they are made by judges of distinguished reputation, are of assistance to courts in later cases, but are never binding; later courts are not under any duty to follow them. An example of this arises where a judge purports to decide a case on a principle really wider than is necessary for the purpose, when he might have decided it on some already recognised but narrower ground. But a reason given by a single judge for his decision is not to be regarded as *obiter* merely because he has given an additional reason in the same judgment, and where several judges reach the same result but for different reasons, the judge in the later case is free to select the correct reason.

Much ingenuity is displayed by the judges and by the legal profession in 'distinguishing' cases, but it must not be assumed that the application of the doctrine of precedent is a purely mechanical one, for judgments are based not on the arithmetical calculation of binding precedents, but on the general principles contained in the case-law as a whole.

In Ireland, this system has been generally adopted in its entirety, for, as will be seen, the separate history of the common law here is a comparatively short one. Until 1849 there was almost no indigenous system of legal education; and before 1827 there were few regular series of Irish law reports. It is said of Lord Manners, who was Chancellor of Ireland in the eighteen twenties, that he once addressed counsel thus: "Are you sure, Mr Plunket, that what you have stated is the law?" "It unquestionably was the law half an hour ago," replied the advocate, pulling out his watch, "but by now the packet boat has probably arrived, and I shall not be positive," meaning, of course, that the arrival of the latest volumes of the law reports from England might have altered the situation.

There is no reference to the doctrine of precedent in either the Constitution of 1922 or the Constitution of 1937, but the changes brought about by the introduction of a written Constitution have raised a number of problems. Prior to 1921, the ultimate tribunal for hearing appeals from Ireland was the House of Lords; and the former Court of Appeal in Ireland evolved a practice with regard to English decisions whereby, though it was not technically bound by the decisions of coordinate English courts, it would, in cases where the law of the two countries was identical, follow them, and leave it to the House of Lords to correct the errors. [1] For its own decisions, the Irish Court of Appeal evolved a system of assembling a full court in order to override a previous decision. [2]

Under the Irish Free State Constitution, article 73, the "laws in force" at the date of its coming into effect were carried over *in toto*, subject to their being consistent with the Constitution, and subject also to their subsequent repeal or amendment. The Constitution of Ireland, 1937, article 50, contains a similar provision. The effect of these provisions were first considered by Gavan Duffy J. in *Exham* v. *Beamish* [3] and he suggested that the 1937 Constitution had the effect of transferring only such pre-1922 decisions as had become accepted in Irish law before 1922. This view did not find universal acceptance amongst the judiciary, however. Thus, in *Boylan* v. *Dublin Corporation* [4] the Supreme Court had to consider the effect of *Fairman* v. *Perpetual Building Society* [5], a decision of the House of Lords given a month before the Irish Free State Constitution came into force. Both Maguire C.J. and Black J. were of opinion that they were bound by the earlier case. Moreover, in *Minister for Finance and Attorney General* v. *O'Brien* [6], a later case, Murnaghan J. said: "... I understand the position, decisions of the House of Lords upon law common to England and Ireland given before the coming into operation of the Constitution of 1922 are of binding force in the Courts until their effect has been altered by the legislature."

In the last decade there has been a trend away from the rigid application of the system of absolutely binding precedents both in the United Kingdom and Ireland. In the *Attorney General and Another v Ryan's Car Hire Ltd.*, [7] the Supreme Court held that it

[1] *McCartan* v. *Belfast Harbour Commissioners* [1910] 2 I.R. 470, 494.
[2] *Milligan* v. *Mayor of Londonderry* [1920] 2 I.R. 1.
[3] [1939] I.R. 336, 348.
[4] [1949] I.R. 60.
[5] [1923] A.C. 74.
[6] [1949] I.R. 91.
[7] [1965] I.R. 642.

was at liberty to refuse to follow its own previous decisions if it
was satisfied that they were clearly wrong.

Equity

We have already seen that the primary sources of the common law
of England were the decisions of the judges declaring what the
general custom of the realm was, and the enacted legislation of
parliament. One of the weaknesses of the system of judicial statement
of the rules of law, however, lay in the fact that certainty was achieved
at the expense of flexibility. At first, it is true, the judges would decide
cases as justice demanded: but after this process had been developed,
it came to be held by the judiciary that it was no part of their function
to do abstract justice in individual cases, but rather to apply the rigid
rule of law to the facts before them. As a result, the merits of the
case might be overlooked, and it might fall to be decided on some
legal technicality. In these circumstances, the practice grew up of
potential litigants petitioning the King in order to avail themselves
of the residue of justice with which he was invested by medieval
political theory.

One of the striking features of the medieval monarchy was that
the King was in a very real sense the ruler of England. He did not
act alone, however, and throughout the period was assisted and
advised by his council, for at a time when the exigencies of war might
require his absence on the continent, it was essential that some body
should exist for the carrying on of government. This council, or the
Curia Regis, as it was called, was dominated by two officials, each
presiding over what would now be called a department. One was
the Treasurer, who controlled the Exchequer. The other was the
Chancellor, who presided over the Chancery or secretarial department. It was to the Chancellor that the King came to refer many
of these petitions submitted to him by discontented subjects. He was
chief adviser to the King, 'the keeper of his conscience', and invariably an ecclesiastic.

Even before this time, the Chancellor had acquired an important
degree of control over the judicial administration of the country. In
order to commence legal proceedings in any of the King's courts, it
was necessary for the litigant to obtain a writ, i.e., a command issued
in the King's name, directing the other party to the dispute to appear
in court to answer the claim. These writs issued out of the Chancery,

and the question as to whether a person had a valid legal claim or not, depended on the fact of there being a writ already in existence to suit that claim. The Chancellor asserted the right to issue writs to meet new cases, sufficiently like those for which writs already existed, and so extend the law, but the common law courts claimed to be capable of deciding whether a writ was good or not. Nevertheless, the Chancellor had assumed an important part in the administration of the business of the courts, and so it was but natural that the King should refer the 'hard cases' to him for adjudication. At first, the Chancellor advised the King on how he should do justice; later, as his jurisdiction developed, he came to decide them on his own.

The sort of case which would come before the Chancellor in this way involved circumstances where the petitioner had suffered a legal wrong, but for some reason could not get redress, either because of his poverty or because of the wealth or political power of his opponent. Again, it might be that the petitioner had entered into a transaction which would give him a moral right to redress, but a right which the common law courts could not protect. The enforcement of what afterwards came to be called 'trusts' fell under this heading. These were transactions where a person transferred the legal title in property to another, charged with the moral obligation to hold it 'on trust' for a third party. Such third-party rights would not be admitted by the common law, but they would be enforced by the Chancellor, on the basis that it would be contrary to conscience and morality to ignore such an obligation.

The remedy afforded by the Chancellor in all these cases was both drastic and effective. He would summon the defendant before him, on pain of forfeiting a sum of money, and examine him on oath. He was not restrained by the technical legal rules of procedure, but would do what was necessary to achieve a just solution to the dispute. He did not reverse the decision of the common law courts, should they have decided the issue in favour of the defendant. What he did was to say that in such circumstances the defendant could not, in equity, make use of his common law rights in order to ignore his moral obligation. And if the defendant refused to obey, the Chancellor would imprison him. He could issue orders compelling defendants to do things or to refrain from doing them, and when he did so, the Chancellor alleged that he was acting in the best interests of the defendant in order to prevent him from violating the dictates of his own conscience.

In this way, the Chancellor gradually acquired a jurisdiction parallel with that of the common law, but independent of it; and that jurisdiction he came to exercise in his own tribunal which was called the Court of Chancery. In this way, too, the collection of miscellaneous notions of 'equity' and 'good conscience', at first applied at random by Chancellors in deciding individual petitions, came to be systematised, and the general 'principles of equity' came to be regarded more and more as definite rules. So there evolved what, in effect, was a separate set of rules which were to be applied uniformly in the future. At first, these rules came into conflict with the common law rules, but the series of disputes which arose between the two systems were eventually resolved in favour of the continued existence of the Court of Chancery.

As this equitable jurisdiction developed, so also did it attract to itself the doctrine of binding precedent, and eventually the advent of a system of reported cases in Chancery ensured that the principles of equity were no longer vague generalisations, but rather a set of rules which could be invoked to supplement the common law. The abolition of the separate Court of Chancery in the nineteenth century did not affect this, and to the present time equity exists and continues to supply an important source of law in this process of supplementation.

Minor Sources of Law

Reference has already been made to the way in which the reported decisions of the courts are used to develop the principles of the common law. In addition to these reported cases, the reports of cases in other jurisdictions—in the United States, in Canada and Australia, and in the courts of England since 1922—can be cited as 'persuasive' authorities, as can the decisions of the courts in Northern Ireland. These last usually possess a high degree of 'persuasion', because of the similarity of the two legal systems in Ireland.

In the systems of law derived from the Roman law, the works of authoritative legal writers form an important source of law, and in Scotland, for example, the so-called 'institutional writers' occupy a special place in the legal system. In Anglo-Irish law, by contrast, very little weight is attached to legal writings. Some of the older books, however, are known as 'books of authority', and will be accepted in the courts. These are works such as Coke's *Institutes* (17th century), Bracton's *De Legibus* (13th century), Littleton's *Tenures* (15th century), Foster's *Crown Law* (18th century) and Blackstone's *Commentaries*, and they carry almost equal weight with reported cases. Some of the earlier law reports, indeed, are of such indifferent accuracy as to be unreliable, and the judges have learnt not to accept them without question. It must be emphasised once again, however, that any report of a decision written down and signed by a member of the Bar will be accepted in the Irish courts.

In recent times, the tradition of not accepting the works of textbook writers in the courts has tended to break down in England, and inroads were made into the rule much earlier in the United States. As a matter of experience, it has been found that the quality of legal writing has improved, and citation is not now confined to textbooks, but extends to articles in legal periodicals as well. By etiquette, counsel who refer to the works of living authors do not cite them directly as authorities, but request the leave of the court to 'adopt' them as part of their argument. In practice, this rule is often disregarded.

In Ireland, it is not so easy to discern this trend with regard to legal textbooks, but the adoption of a fairly rigid written Constitution in 1937 has resulted in more attention being paid by the courts to the decisions on constitutional questions of the courts in the United States, Canada and Australia. At first, such citation was very tentative, and frequently the existence of the most recent cases was not revealed to the courts, but one now can see an increasing tendency to draw upon these foreign storehouses of legal learning and judicial opinion.

CHAPTER II

THE BACKGROUND OF THE IRISH JUDICIAL SYSTEM

In order to determine the origin of the existing courts of law in Ireland, it is necessary to investigate their predecessors; and this, in turn, leads to an examination of the steps by which the common law came to be introduced into Ireland. Since that law was engrafted on the newly-conquered territory *de novo*, and was not an amalgam of any pre-existing system with a body of law, it follows that we must consider the system of courts operating in England at the time of its arrival in Ireland.

Attention has already been drawn to the fact that the Norman kings ruled England with the assistance of a council called the *Curia Regis*, or King's Court. This council was not a 'court' in the modern sense of the term, but was rather a general body of royal officials assembled to assist the sovereign. With the passage of time, these meetings of the *Curia Regis* tended to break down into two types. There were the great assemblies of all the advisers, held periodically, and there were the smaller 'committee' meetings of officials, held more frequently. These smaller meetings of officials became formalised; they accumulated staffs around them, and, gradually, they tended to develop into separate institutions, administrative and judicial. It is from these smaller bodies that can be traced the development of the Royal Courts. Even before that development, however, there was in existence another judicial institution, that of the itinerant justices.

From the time of the Norman Conquest, there is evidence of the fact that royal commissioners were sent around England in order to perform governmental functions in the King's name. The nature of these functions was determined by the commission under which they were empowered to act, and though they were often entrusted with judicial functions, they were given other tasks as well. Soon, however, it became the practice to send out regular judicial commissions to hear and decide criminal cases within a defined area. These were the 'Commission of Oyer and Terminer' and the 'Commission of Gaol Delivery.'

In addition, it became the practice to issue a 'Commission of Assize', whereby the commissioners were empowered to hear all the civil as well as the criminal cases pending before the Royal Courts at Westminster at the time they came into the county for which the Commission issued. This was designed to convenience litigants, and to spare them the journey to Westminster. Such local hearings came to be known as 'hearings at *nisi prius*', from the language of the statute (Statute of Westminster II, 1285) which provided that all civil cases were to be tried at Westminster, "Unless the itinerant justices have come before into those parts." By the end of the thirteenth century, then, the royal justices were travelling through England twice a year, deciding cases, and this practice is adhered to in both England and Northern Ireland to the present day.

It remains to describe very briefly the various courts that evolved from the *Curia Regis*.

The Court of Exchequer

It has already been pointed out that the Exchequer, presided over by the Treasurer, was one of the earliest departments of state to be evolved from the council; and it soon split into two sides, an administrative and a judicial side. In its earlier stages, the judicial side was concerned with disputes which arose in connection with the royal revenues. It was presided over by a Chief Baron, who was assisted by a number of *puisne*, or inferior barons. As its jurisdiction evolved, it acquired new judicial tasks, for it came to be held that a plaintiff might resort to the Court of Exchequer, and obtain financial redress against his adversary, if he could allege that he was indebted to the Crown, and so was seeking payment from the defendant in order to discharge his public obligation. This allegation, in the course of time, became a pure fiction, but it served to enable the court to acquire jurisdiction—an important consideration at a time when the barons were remunerated out of the fees of litigants.

The Court of Common Pleas

In order to relieve the pressure of business on the *Curia Regis* in dispensing royal justice, Henry II deputed five officials of his council to sit permanently at Westminster in order to hear pleas, or civil actions, between his subjects, who were thus spared the task of having to pursue the King on his progress through the country. This body became the Court of Common Pleas, sometimes called the Common Bench. A Chief Justice of the Common Pleas was at its head, assisted by a staff of *puisne* judges.

The Court of King's Bench

After the Exchequer and the Common Pleas had broken away from the *Curia Regis*, the parent body continued to exercise judicial functions, and a distinction came to be drawn between the Common Pleas on the one hand and the Court *coram rege* on the other. Soon a Chief Justice of the King's Bench was appointed—also assisted by *puisnes*—and this part of the council evolved into a separate court.

The Court of King's Bench, being more intimately connected with the Sovereign, remained the most important of the three common law courts. It tried criminal cases—though, as we have seen, many of these would come before the itinerant justices. Moreover, it exercised a concurrent jurisdiction with the Common Pleas in civil cases, and its procedure was more expeditious. Finally, it exercised a supervisory jurisdiction over inferior tribunals by means of the so-called 'prerogative writs' which issued from it.

The Court of Chancery

In the first chapter we described the part played by equity in the development of the common law, and the way in which the Court of Chancery, which evolved these principles, came into existence.

*   *   *

THE INTRODUCTION OF THE COMMON LAW INTO IRELAND

Although Richard FitzGilbert, Earl of Pembroke and usually known as 'Strongbow', led the Normans to Ireland as early as 1170, the reception of the English system of courts of law was a very gradual process. In its initial stages, the government of the country was assigned to a Justiciar, or permanent deputy who, from the beginning of the thirteenth century, was dispensing royal justice in his master's name, through the medium of the royal writs. Assizes were held in Ireland; the jury system was introduced; and

Englishmen were appointed to judicial office in the country, thus speeding up the process of development.

The idea that the law used in Ireland should be identical with that of England was declared in express terms; this is apparent from the fact that when King John visited Ireland in 1210 he ordered that the laws and customs of England were to be observed in Ireland. It must be emphasised, however, that the application of the common law was by no means general, and was confined to English settlers and to the area of the Pale, around Dublin, occupied by the colonists. As a general rule, the native Irish were not admitted to the advantages of the new law. Outside the Pale, they retained their native *brehon* law, a system which was not finally displaced until the seventeenth century, despite continuous efforts at its suppression, accompanied by statements to the effect that the Irish laws were 'so contrary to all law that they ought not to be deemed laws.' In the early thirteenth century, moreover, it became common to grant by charter to individual Irishmen or groups of them the right to use English law.

Within the Pale the native Irish were, under the feudal system pertaining there, reduced to the status of villeins or what were called *betaghs*. This was a pre-Norman status in Ireland, meaning one who was attached to the soil, and the Normans adapted it to their legal needs in order to enable an Irishman to sue in the Royal Courts if he were injured by his feudal lords. During the period 1277–1280, efforts were made to extend the common law to the Irish generally, but nothing came of it, and it was not until 1331 that Irishmen, other than *betaghs*, became entitled to use English law.

The precise relationship existing between the common law and the older *brehon* law outside the Pale is still a matter for conjecture, and the documentary evidence available is so scanty that our knowledge is unlikely to be increased. In 1558, for instance, the Privy Council of Ireland ordered a dispute involving title to land to be decided by *brehons*.

Finally, in the seventeenth century, due mainly to the energies of the Irish Attorney General, Sir John Davies, the common law came to be extended to the whole country. Two decisions of the King's Bench in the reign of James I practically destroyed the whole structure of the customary system of land tenure: one of these declared that the *brehon* law custom of gavelkind succession was illegal, while the other condemned the allied custom of 'tanistry.'

As late as the beginning of the seventeenth century, however, there are occasional references in the State Papers to the native 'regions', which show the survival of the old law there. In 1612, the Irish Parliament passed a statute[1] reciting that ". . . all the natives and inhabitants of this kingdom, without difference and distinction, are taken into his Majestie's gratious protection, and doe now live under one law as dutiful subjects of our Soveraigne Lord and Monarch."

The stages by which the common law system of courts was set up in Ireland followed closely on the English development. As in England, the *Curia Regis* was the chief source, and the King was represented by the Justiciar. On his journeys through the country he was accompanied by professional justices. After the visit of Richard II to Ireland in 1394–95, this court became the Irish Court of King's Bench. The Exchequer and the Common Pleas developed in the thirteenth century, while the Court of Chancery emerged at a later date.

In addition to the importation of the principles of the common law and a developing system of equity, repeated attempts were made to apply the statutes of the Parliament of England to Ireland. The validity of such a process seems to have been denied by the English judges in the reign of Henry VI, though in a later case, after two hearings, the opposite conclusion was reached.[2] The statute known as Poynings' Act 1494–95[3] attempted to remove doubts by declaring that all statutes previously made by the English Parliament should have full effect in Ireland. This controversy concerning the claim of the English Parliament to legislate for Ireland, together with the allied claim of the English House of Lords to exercise appellate jurisdiction from Irish courts (of which more hereafter) continued through the seventeenth and eighteenth centuries. By a statute of the Irish Parliament, called Yelverton's Act 1781–82[4], there were extended to Ireland "all statutes heretofore made in England or Great Britain" for settling forfeited estates; or concerning commerce; seamen; the style or calendar; the taking of oaths; or continuance of any office, commission or writ, etc., in case of a demise of the Crown. Finally, by the Act of Union 1800, which was enacted by

[1] 11, 12 & 13 Jac. I c. 5.
[2] *Case of the Merchants of Waterford*, Y.B. Ric. III f. 12; Y.B. 1 Hen. VII f. 2 (1483–4).
[3] 10 Hen. VII c. 22 (Ir.).
[4] 21 & 22 Geo. III c. 48 (Ir.).

parallel statutes of 39 & 40 Geo. III c. 67 in Great Britain, and 40 Geo. III c. 38 (Ir.) in Ireland, "all laws in force at the time of the Union, and all the courts of civil and ecclesiastical jurisdiction within the respective Kingdoms, shall remain as now by law established within the same, subject only to such alterations and regulations from time to time as circumstances may appear to the Parliament of the United Kingdom to require." This provision secured the continuance of the law in Ireland as enacted by pre-Union Irish Parliaments.

CHAPTER III

THE SYSTEM OF COURTS IN IRELAND 1800-1921

It will be convenient to pause at the date of the Act of Union 1800, and to examine the hierarchy of courts existing at that time, for, by then, the Irish judicial system had assumed the form it was to retain until the constitutional settlement of 1920–1922.

The Superior Courts

There were six superior courts in Dublin. As we have already seen, four of them—the Exchequer, the Common Pleas, the King's Bench, and the Court of Chancery—had been evolved in the medieval period. The Court of Exchequer was headed by the Lord Chief Baron, assisted by three *puisne* barons. The Court of Common Pleas had a Lord Chief Justice of the Common Pleas and three *puisne* judges. The Court of King's Bench was headed by a Lord Chief Justice, generally termed the 'Lord Chief Justice of Ireland', and assisted by three *puisne* judges. In the Court of Chancery, the Lord Chancellor presided alone, though by a statute of 1801[1] the Master of the Rolls was made a judge and assigned to assist in the Chancery work.

The remaining two courts were more recent in origin. The Court of Prerogative and Faculties—an ecclesiastical court with jurisdiction over wills—claimed to exercise jurisdiction by virtue of two sixteenth-century statutes[2] and two seventeenth-century patents, one of James I and the other of Charles I. The High Court of Admiralty had been created by a statute in 1784[3] though there had

[1] 41 Geo. III c. 25.
[2] 28 Hen. VIII c. 19; Eliz. I c. 1.
[3] 23 & 24 Geo. III c. 14 (Ir.).

been an admiralty jurisdiction exercised in Ireland from medieval times.

The position regarding appeals was a little complicated. All the courts mentioned above had 'original jurisdiction', i.e. jurisdiction to try cases at first instance; in some circumstances, they also had jurisdiction 'in error', to review the decision of other tribunals. Apart from the cases where, in order to avoid a miscarriage of justice, a new trial might be ordered, there was until 1877 no general right of 'appeal' in the modern sense of the term. The only way to challenge a decision of one of the common law courts was by 'writ of error', alleging that there was some defect on the 'record' of the case, i.e., in the pleadings, the issue, or the verdict. Any error outside the 'record', e.g., a jury misdirection, could not be questioned.

In this sense, 'error' lay from the Court of Common Pleas in Ireland to the Irish King's Bench, while 'error' from the Irish King's Bench lay to the King's Bench in England. In addition, a writ of error was at one time taken from the King's Bench in Ireland to the Irish House of Lords, but at that time a writ of error would lie from the Irish House of Lords to the King's Bench in England.

The practice of appealing directly from the Irish Courts to the English House of Lords seems to have originated in appeals from the Irish Court of Chancery. The Irish House of Lords claimed the right to act as the final appellate tribunal for Ireland. After the accession of George I, this conflict of jurisdiction reached its most acute stage. In the case of *Annesley* v. *Sherlock*, which came before the Irish Court of Exchequer, appeals were taken both to the Irish House of Lords and to the English House of Lords. These tribunals gave conflicting judgments which neither would retract. The result was a declaratory statute of the Parliament of Great Britain, 6 Geo. I c. 19,1719, affirming that the Irish House of Lords had no jurisdiction to determine Irish appeals.

The British statute of 1719 remained in force until 1782, when it was repealed by 22 Geo. III c. 53. This restored all the doubts of the position before 1719, and a further statute was passed—23 Geo. III c. 28—which, while it did not confer appellate jurisdiction on the Irish House of Lords, excluded the English courts from hearing Irish appeals. Here the position remained, with the Irish House of Lords as the final court of appeal, until the Act of Union, when Irish appeals were directed to go to the House of Lords of the United Kingdom of Great Britain and Ireland.

So far as the Court of Exchequer was concerned, appeal in error lay to a special court, called the 'Court of Exchequer Chamber', set up in Ireland under the authority of an English statute, 31 Edw. III, st. 1, c. 12, 1357–58, and consisting of the Lord Chancellor, the Lord Treasurer and the other judges. Later statutes regulated the composition of this court, and it is thought that appeals from it would lie to the House of Lords in England. There was no statute in Ireland corresponding to the English 27 Eliz. I c. 8, 1585, and providing for the hearing of error from the Irish King's Bench; this, as has been seen, went directly to the King's Bench in England. In 1800, the Irish Parliament, by the statute 40 Geo. III c. 39 (Ir.), created a new Court of Exchequer Chamber, consisting of the two Chief Justices, the Chief Baron, and all the *puisne* justices and barons, with a quorum of nine. It was to hear appeals in error from the King's Bench, Common Pleas, and the common law side of the Exchequer, and such common law jurisdiction as was possessed by the Court of Chancery. Finally, by the statute 21 & 22 Vic. c. 6, 1857, it was provided that the Court should be constituted by the judges other than those from which the appeal was taken.

From the High Court of Admiralty, an appeal lay under the statute of 1784 to the Delegates in Chancery, and a similar practice obtained in the Court of Prerogative and Faculties. In 1856, however, a new Court—the 'Court of Appeal in Chancery'—was set up, with a Lord Justice of Appeal in Chancery; it heard appeals from the Lord Chancellor (who might sit with the Lord Justice), the Master of Rolls, and the High Court of Admiralty. From thence, appeals went to the House of Lords, except in the case of admiralty suits, which went to the Irish Privy Council. [4]

In addition to the regulation of appeals, nineteenth-century legislation created a number of other courts for Ireland. The Incumbered Estates Court, consisting of three commissioners (of which one was an Exchequer baron), was set up in 1849, under 12 & 13 Vic. c. 77, with an appeal to the Irish Privy Council. This was intended to be a temporary tribunal, but in 1858 it was made permanent, as the Landed Estates Court, under 21 & 22 Vic. c. 72, with

[4] 19 & 20 Vic. c. 92.

an appeal to the Court of Appeal in Chancery. It was composed of three and later of two judges, whose status was equivalent to those of a common law judge. [5] An appeal lay to the Court of Appeal in Chancery.

In 1818 the Court for the Relief of Insolvent Debtors was set up, composed of two Commissioners. [6] Under two statutes of 1836 and 1837 [7], two permanent Commissioners in Bankruptcy were appointed, and in 1857 the Court of Bankruptcy and Insolvency was established, consisting of two judges, with an appeal to the Court of Appeal in Chancery. [8]

In 1848 'The Court of Crown Cases Reserved' was set up, consisting of all the judges of the common law courts, solely to hear questions of law which might be reserved at any criminal trial under a commission of oyer and terminer and gaol delivery. This jurisdiction was continued after the Judicature (Ir.) Act 1877, five judges of the High Court forming a quorum, and their decision was final. It was a statutory recognition of what had long been an informal practice of judges in criminal trials.

The testamentary jurisdiction of the old Court of Prerogative and Faculties was transferred to a new court, the Court of Probate, in 1857, with an appeal to the Court of Appeal in Chancery [9], while in 1870 the disestablishment of the Church of Ireland resulted in the matrimonial jurisdiction of the ecclesiastical courts being transferred to the Court of Matrimonial Causes and Matters, the probate judge being also the judge of this court. [10] Appeal lay to the Court of Appeal in Chancery.

It should be noted that the Court of Chancery was reinforced in 1867 by the appointment of Vice-Chancellor with concurrent jurisdiction with the Lord Chancellor [11] and, in the same year the High Court of Admiralty was reorganised with one judge only, [12] with appeal to the Court of Appeal in Chancery and to the Irish Privy Council.

[5] 29 & 30 Vic. c. 99.
[6] 1 & 2 Geo. IV c. 59.
[7] 6 Will. IV c. 14; 1 Vic. c. 8.
[8] 20 & 21 Vic. c. 60.
[9] 20 & 21 Vic. c. 79.
[10] 33 & 34 Vic. c. 110.
[11] 30 & 31 Vic. c. 44.
[12] 30 & 31 Vic. c. 114.

The Judicature (Ireland) Act 1877

This statute, modelled on equivalent legislation passed for England in 1873–75, effected a radical change in the judicial organisation of the Irish courts. It provided that the Courts of Chancery, Queen's Bench, Common Pleas, Exchequer, Probate, Matrimonial Causes and Matters, Admiralty, and the Landed Estates Court were to be fused into one court, called 'The Supreme Court of Judicature in Ireland', and that this court was to administer equity and the common law concurrently. The Supreme Court of Judicature was to have two permanent divisions, the High Court of Justice, with original jurisdiction and power to hear appeals from courts of local jurisdiction, and the Court of Appeal, exercising appellate jurisdiction. The Court of Appeal consisted of the Lord Chancellor, the Master of the Rolls, the Lord Chief Justice of Ireland, the Chief Justice of the Common Pleas, the Chief Baron of the Exchequer, and two other judges known as 'Lord Justices of Appeal.' The High Court consisted of the members of the Courts of Appeal, save the Lord Justices, and eleven other judges.

For the more convenient dispatch of business, the High Court was divided into five divisions—Chancery (including the Land Judge), Queen's Bench, Common Pleas, Exchequer, Probate and Matrimonial, and, on the death of the existing judge, the Admiralty was also to be merged with the High Court, an event which occurred in 1893. In 1887, the Common Pleas Division was merged with the Queen's Bench Division, the office of Chief Justice of the Common Pleas lapsing[13], and in 1897 the Exchequer Division and the Probate Division were also merged with the Queen's Bench, which also extinguished the Court of Bankruptcy when the last judge of that Court was appointed to the Queen's Bench.[14] In 1903 the office of Vice-Chancellor was not filled on the resignation of the holder and a judge was transferred from the King's Bench Division to sit in the Chancery Division. In 1906 the vacancy so created in the King's Bench was filled, but the Judicature (Ir.) Act 1907 provided that the next two vacancies in the King's Bench Division were not to be filled.

The position, then, in 1921 was that there was a Court of Appeal composed of six judges, and a High Court comprising a Chancery

[13] 50 Vic. c. 6.
[14] 60 & 61 Vic. c. 66.

Division of four judges and a King's Bench Division of eight judges. To these should be added the two Judicial Commissioners of the Court of the Irish Land Commission, the first being appointed under the Land Law (Ir.) Act 1881, and the second under the Irish Land Act 1903.

The table opposite will illustrate the structure of the superior courts in Ireland between the Act of Union 1800 and 1921.

The Assize System

In an earlier chapter, reference was made to the fact that one of the characteristics of the common law as it was administered in England was the sending out of judges to the counties at stated intervals, on Commissions of Assize, charged with the duty of 'delivering the gaols' and also with the business of trying civil actions at *nisi prius*. With the introduction of the common law into Ireland, this system was carried on and itinerant justices were traversing the country on commissions of oyer and terminer and gaol delivery in the thirteenth century. As early as 1570, Assizes were being held in the counties of Dublin, Kildare, Carlow, Kilkenny, Louth, Meath, Westmeath, Longford and in King's County, and by 1610, Assizes covered the whole country. In the summer of 1614 there appeared laid out for the judges five circuits, embracing the thirty-two counties. At first, only part of the country was travelled in the spring Assizes, but in 1617 the same circuits were assigned as in the summer.

These circuits were five in number, a sixth being added in 1796. The North-East covered Meath, Louth, Monaghan, Armagh, Down, Antrim and (later) the City of Belfast. The North-West included Westmeath, Longford, Cavan, Fermanagh, Tyrone, Donegal and Londonderry. The Connaught Circuit was King's County, Leitrim, Sligo, Roscommon, Mayo and Galway. In the Leinster Circuit there were Tipperary, Queen's County, Waterford, Kilkenny, Carlow, Kildare, Wexford and Wicklow. Munster embraced Clare, Limerick, Kerry and Cork. In addition, after 1876, a winter Assize, for criminal business only, was held in some convenient Assize town for each province. In 1796, the sixth circuit, the Home, was carved out of the others, and included Meath, Westmeath, Carlow, Kildare, King's County and Queen's County. This circuit was abolished after a further reorganisation in 1885.

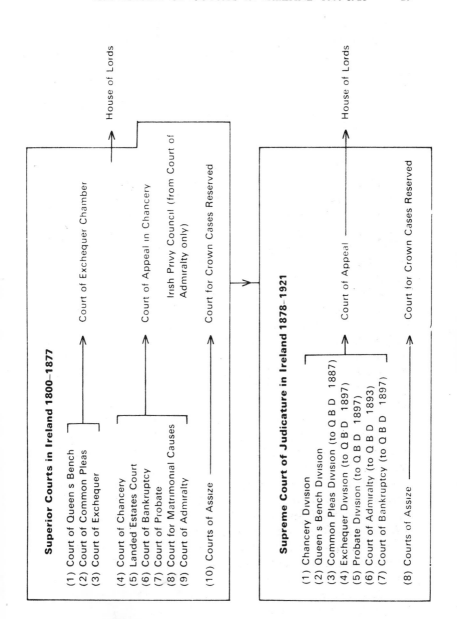

Superior Courts in Ireland 1800–1877

(1) Court of Queen s Bench
(2) Court of Common Pleas
(3) Court of Exchequer

Court of Exchequer Chamber → House of Lords

(4) Court of Chancery
(5) Landed Estates Court
(6) Court of Bankruptcy
(7) Court of Probate
(8) Court for Matrimonial Causes
(9) Court of Admiralty

Court of Appeal in Chancery

Irish Privy Council (from Court of Admiralty only)

(10) Courts of Assize

Court for Crown Cases Reserved

Supreme Court of Judicature in Ireland 1878–1921

(1) Chancery Division
(2) Queen s Bench Division
(3) Common Pleas Division (to Q B D 1887)
(4) Exchequer Division (to Q B D 1897)
(5) Probate Division (to Q B D 1897)
(6) Court of Admiralty (to Q B D 1893)
(7) Court of Bankruptcy (to Q B D 1897)

Court of Appeal → House of Lords

(8) Courts of Assize

Court for Crown Cases Reserved

For the County of the City of Dublin there was a permanent Commission, sitting at Green Street Courthouse and presided over by one of the Queen's Bench judges, selected by rota. It sat six times a year, in the months of February, April, June, August, October and December, and tried indictable crime arising within the area of the city. All the judges of the Queen's Bench, together with the Lord Mayor of Dublin, were named in this Commission and, in addition, a second Commission issued (to the judges alone) for the County of Dublin.

The Courts of Local Jurisdiction
Justices of the Peace

In the development of the law in England, the work of the itinerant justices became too heavy for them to cope with, because of the increasing range of crimes. In addition, the extension of the civil business of the courts led to an increase of trials at *nisi prius*. The need to deal with the growing volume of crime led, in England, to the creation of the office of Justice of the Peace. A statute of 1327 made provision for the appointment of 'conservators of the peace' for each English county, and these came to be known as 'justices of the peace.' At first their duty was confined to bringing offenders before the judges of Assize, but by a statute of 1345 they were given power to punish offenders themselves. In 1361 a special commission was assigned to each county, to include persons "learned in the law" who would preserve the peace.

From about 1363 in England, these justices seem to have met four times a year in 'Quarter Sessions' and to have investigated offences alleged to have been committed. Much of their work was of an administrative nature. By a statute of 1590 they were empowered to inquire into all offences, with the proviso that difficult cases should be reserved for Assizes. In the course of time, this jurisdiction was extended by the creation of new offences by statute, but certain serious crimes were excluded from their jurisdiction. In Ireland, fewer offences were excluded from Quarter Sessions and, in theory, the justices had a wide jurisdiction. In practice, government circulars excluded from their jurisdiction cases of treason, murder, felonies punishable by penal servitude for life, and "all felonies of a political and insurrectionary character."

The jurisdiction of justices in 'Petty Sessions' seems to have been built up by statute and usage. Many statutes gave justices or any two of them jurisdiction to deal with offences 'out of sessions', and these sittings out of (Quarter) sessions came to be known as Petty Sessions.

In Ireland, the development appears to have been along similar lines. An Irish statute of 1351 provided for the appointment of four guardians of the peace for each county; their chief function appears to have been the suppression of 'the Irish enemies.' They are first described as Justices of the Peace in the statute 11 Hen. IV (Ir.), 1410. The disturbed state of the country in the ensuing centuries must have inhibited the proper development of a system of Quarter Sessions, but by the end of the seventeenth century it seems to have been worked out for most counties.

In addition to trying offences of what would now be called a summary nature (a jurisdiction which was entirely statutory), justices were charged with the duty of conducting 'out of sessions' the preliminary examination of criminals who were to be tried on Assize. At first, this investigation was inquisitorial in character, and the accused person was not present when the witnesses were examined. In the nineteenth century, however, a series of statutes dating from 1827 were passed, with the object of regularising this procedure and preventing abuses. The justice had to decide on the sufficiency of the evidence offered and either discharge the prisoner or return him for trial at Quarter Sessions or at the Assizes. If he was returned for trial, a 'bill of indictment', setting out the charge against him, was preferred to the Grand Jury by the prosecutor, who was usually the Attorney General, or counsel representing the Crown. The Grand Jury thereupon determined whether the bill was a 'true bill' or not. If they considered that there was a prima facie case, they returned a 'true bill'; if not, they 'ignored' it. When a true bill was found, it thereupon became an indictment, triable by a Petty Jury, at Assize or Quarter Sessions.

The system of unpaid magistrates, or justices, did not work satisfactorily in Ireland, for it was from time to time alleged that unsuitable persons were being appointed to the bench. Petty Sessions were not held regularly in this country before 1827, when provision was made for regular sessions with a paid clerk. Moreover, most of the efforts made by successive governments to strengthen this branch of the judiciary failed, and so the expedient was tried of supplementing them with whole-time magistrates. Under the statute 33 Geo. III c. 36 (Ir.) 1795, provision was made for the appointment of stipendiary magistrates for the City of Dublin, who controlled the city constabulary and exercised the powers of the justices of the peace. In 1814, the Lord Lieutenant was empowered to proclaim an area to be in a state of disturbance and to appoint for it 'magistrates of police', with the powers of a justice. Each of these was to head a force of constabulary.[15] In 1822, the Lord Lieutenant was given power, on the application of the justices of the county, to appoint salaried magistrates who would be permanently resident in their districts.[16] These magistrates were not to be connected with the police. Finally, in 1836, the police forces in Ireland were organised on a national basis, called the 'Constabulary of Ireland' (later called the Royal Irish Constabulary), and the statute carrying out this reform[17] empowered the appointment of 'resident magistrates.' These were to reside in their districts, were not to hold office in the constabulary, and were to report regularly to the Chief Secretary on the state of their districts. This power was extensively employed, and by 1912 there were sixty-four resident magistrates, covering the whole country outside Dublin.

In their judicial powers, however, the resident magistrates had no more authority than a justice of the peace, and at Petty Sessions the bench might often be composed of stipendiary and lay magistrates.

The County Courts

Unlike the rest of the pre-1921 judicial system in Ireland, the system of County Courts had no exact parallel in England. The English system of County Courts was developed at the beginning of the nineteenth century in order to deal with small cases; before that time the only way in which a civil case could be tried outside London was by a judge of Assize sitting at *nisi prius*. In Ireland, the local jurisdiction was developed along different lines, and is very closely connected with a form of procedure peculiar to Ireland known as the 'civil bill.' This practice seems to have existed in England in medieval times, in connection with the older County Courts, but while it was supplanted there by the writ in the case

[15] 54 Geo. III c. 131.
[16] 3 Geo. IV c. 103.
[17] 6 & 7 Will. IV c. 13.

of the Royal Courts, it survived in Ireland. Because it was free from technicality, the procedure by bill was cheaper and more expeditious than the procedure by writ in civil actions, and it became very popular. From the seventeenth century onwards, the practice arose of including in the Commission of Assize power to try actions in Ireland by bill as well as by writ and this continued into the following century. By 1796, the volume of cases being decided in this way was so large that it was thought necessary to relieve the judges of Assize of the work. In County Dublin, civil bills had for some time been heard at Quarter Sessions. Under the statute 36 Geo. III c. 25 (Ir.) 1796, in each county a barrister of six years' standing was appointed to act as assistant to the justices of Quarter Sessions, and this 'assistant barrister', as he was called, was empowered to hear civil bills as the sole and exclusive judge. At first his jurisdiction was limited to the sum of £20 in cases of debt, but during the nineteenth century this amount was increased. A statute of 1851[18] made the assistant barrister Chairman of Quarter Sessions, and he could act in the absence of the lay justices. Finally, in 1877, the assistant barrister was abolished and replaced by a County Court judge, who also became Chairman of Quarter Sessions.

Other Local Courts

In addition to the courts of local and limited jurisdiction already described, there were throughout Ireland a whole series of miscellaneous tribunals, varying with regard to jurisdiction and powers, and having their origins in the charters under which cities, boroughs and manors had been created. After the reform of the Irish municipal corporations in 1840, most of the city and borough courts were abolished, but Dublin, Galway and Carrickfergus retained their Court of Quarter Sessions and Recorder's Court for the trial of civil cases, and the Crown was empowered to grant such courts to any borough which petitioned for them. Where there were Recorders— Dublin, Cork, Belfast, Londonderry, Galway and Carrickfergus— Quarter Sessions were held before them, sitting as sole judges.

Appeals

The system of appeals from courts of local or limited jurisdiction in Ireland before 1921 was, in the main, governed by statute. Thus,

[18] 14 & 15 Vic. c. 57.

many statutes creating offences gave an express right of appeal from Petty Sessions to Quarter Sessions. In the same way, an appeal lay from the court of the assistant barrister, or County Court, to the going judge of Assize, where the civil bill was reheard.

The Queen's Bench Division, as successor to the old Court of Queen's Bench, exercised an extensive supervisory jurisdiction over all inferior tribunals by means of the prerogative writs of *Mandamus*, *Prohibition*, and *Certiorari*. In addition, the Queen's Bench Division claimed the right to review the decisions of justices sitting in Quarter Sessions. This arose out of the express terms of the Commission of the Peace, which directed the justices named therein to take the opinion of the judges of Assize in cases of difficulty or doubt. Justices sitting at Petty Sessions were also given a statutory power to state a case for the determination of the High Court, on any point of law arising before them.

Binding to the Peace

One of the most important powers conferred on justices of the peace was that which enabled them to require any person to find security to keep the peace or to be of good behaviour, and to order that in default such person be committed to prison. The English statute of 1361,[19] which was extended to Ireland by Poynings' Act, provided that justices should have power to take security from "all them that be not of good fame", while the Commission of the Peace itself recited that the justice on whom it was conferred had been appointed to keep the peace in the county concerned, "and to cause to come before you or any of you all those persons who shall threaten any of our people in their person, or with burning of their houses, to find sufficient security for the peace, or for their good behaviour towards us and our people."

"Security for good behaviour" included "security for the peace", but was much more comprehensive; and the person bound to be of good behaviour was more strictly bound than to the peace, for the peace was not broken without actual violence, whereas behaviour extended to acts which were not criminal. Before 1921, an order binding over was not appealable, but it could be made the subject of a case stated.

Since the Commission of the Peace included the names of all the

[19] 34 Edw. III c. 1.

judges of the superior courts, they also had the power to bind over, and the judges of the Court of King's Bench always claimed the inherent right to exercise this jurisdiction, independently of the statute of 34 Edw. III c. 1.

CHAPTER IV

THE CONSTITUTIONAL CHANGES 1921-1924

The Government of Ireland Act 1920

This legislation was the last of a series of attempts to reconcile the essential unity of the United Kingdom of Great Britain and Ireland, established by the Act of Union 1800, with nationalist aspirations in Ireland. It divided the island into two political units, to be called Northern Ireland and Southern Ireland, each with its own bicameral legislature and judicial system. Certain matters were to be excepted from the local jurisdiction of these legislatures, and other matters were to be reserved to the Imperial Parliament until "the date of Irish union" and were not to be transferred to Irish control until they could be administered on an all-Ireland basis.

The federal structure created by this statute necessitated the creation of separate Supreme Courts of Judicature for Northern Ireland and Southern Ireland, each consisting of a High Court and a Court of Appeal. In addition, a new court, the High Court of Appeal for Ireland, was to act as an appellate court for both jurisdictions; it was to consist of the Lord Chancellor of Ireland, and the Lord Chief Justices of Northern and Southern Ireland, together with additional judges as the occasion demanded. Appeals were to lie from this court to the House of Lords. This court first sat on 15 December 1921, and held its last sitting on 5 December 1922. 'Southern Ireland' never had more than a nominal existence and the Act of 1920 proved to be unworkable in this area. It still forms the basis of the judicial system in Northern Ireland, but the High Court of Appeal was abolished by the Irish Free State (Consequential Provisions) Act 1922, schedule I, para. 6. This Act also repealed the Government of Ireland Act 1920 in so far as it applied to any part of Ireland other than Northern Ireland.

It must be borne in mind, however, that despite the fact that the 1920 Act was ultimately rendered inoperative in the twenty-six county area, nevertheless the necessary steps were taken to bring it into force there. Thus, 1 October 1921 was fixed as the date on which the new system of courts was to become effective in both areas,[1] and on that date, accordingly, the old Supreme Court of Judicature in Ireland ceased to exist, and was replaced by the new Supreme Court of Judicature in Southern Ireland. This had important consequences in the later development of the courts in the Irish Free State.

The Legal Origin of the Irish Free State

One of the difficulties arising out of any attempt to describe the juridical basis of the Irish Free State is that there is, as between British and Irish constitutional theorists, no focus of agreement, in law, as to the exact sequence of events.

According to the Irish view, the State was established on 21 January 1919. On that date, the first assembly of Dáil Éireann, consisting of the majority of those elected for Irish constituencies in the 1918 general election, met in Dublin. On behalf of the Irish people, it formally reaffirmed the Proclamation of the Irish Republic on Easter Monday 1916 and claimed international recognition for the independence of Ireland. In 1921, the argument runs, this republic was recognised by the British government, which negotiated the Anglo-Irish Treaty on 6 December 1921, whereby it was agreed that Ireland should become a dominion, subject to the right of Northern Ireland to opt out of the arrangement. This Treaty was ratified by the Second Dáil and by the Imperial Parliament. The Third Dáil then drafted a constitution which was enacted by that Dáil, sitting as a 'constituent assembly', as the Constitution of the Irish Free State (*Saorstát Éireann*) Act 1922. This was an entirely Irish product, and no British law was in force in Ireland after 1919, except in so far as it was incorporated therein by the Constitution. The validity of the Constitution depended on Irish national sovereignty. The Imperial Parliament, it is true, enacted the Irish Free State (Constitution) Act 1922, but this was entirely a domestic affair in Great Britain; it did not involve Ireland. Moreover, under the provisions of the Irish constituent Act, the

[1] S.R. & O. No. 1527, 1921.

Treaty was given the force of law in the Irish Free State, and any constitutional provision or law repugnant thereto was to be void.

The British view of these events was entirely different. It regarded the First Dáil as a treasonable conspiracy, resulting in armed, but unsuccessful, rebellion. At no time did this illegal assembly exercise *de facto*, much less *de jure*, sovereignty over Irish territory. In 1921, as a matter of political expediency, it was decided to negotiate with these rebels, and the result was the Treaty. According to this view, these negotiations were conducted with certain persons who *happened* to be members of the Parliament of Southern Ireland, and who had been elected thereto under the 1920 Act. (The revolutionaries had used the machinery of elections set up under the 1920 Act to elect to membership of the Second Dáil.) With these persons was signed an *agreement*, not a *treaty*, expressing the intention of the British signatories to take such steps as might be necessary to establish the Irish Free State. This agreement provided for the setting up of a 'provisional government' in Southern Ireland to carry on the administration pending the establishment of the Irish Free State, and, in accordance with its terms, it was ratified by the members elected to serve in the Parliament of Southern Ireland. Further, the Imperial Parliament passed the Irish Free State (Agreement) Act 1922, which in British legal theory gave the force of law to the agreement (the Treaty). This Act gave no recognition to the Second Dáil, or to the Dáil ministry, but made provision for the dissolution of the Parliament of Southern Ireland and for the holding of elections to constitute a new Parliament to which the provisional government should be responsible; further, it provided that that Parliament should, "as respects matters within the jurisdiction of the Provisional Government, have power to make laws in like manner as the Parliament of the Irish Free State when constituted." The Constitution was then drafted by the Irish committee and enacted by the Imperial Parliament in the Irish Free State (Constitution) Act 1922. The Constitution of the Irish Free State (*Saorstát Éireann*) Act 1922 passed by the Third Dáil was enacted as a schedule to this Imperial statute, and was therein described as a 'measure', *not* an 'Act.' Thus, on this view, the whole legal basis of the Irish Free State was to be derived from Imperial legislation, and all the Parliament elected under the Irish Free State (Agreement) Act 1922 (which regarded itself as the Third Dáil) had done was to *prepare* a Constitution, in

accordance with the precedents in Canada, Australia, and South
Africa. The Parliament at Westminster gave it the force of law.

We are not here concerned with the constitutional implications of
these two divergent theories, but from the point of view of the
judicial system, it should be observed that the Irish Free State
(Agreement) Act 1922 enabled transfers to be made by Order in
Council to the provisional government of such powers and machinery
as might be necessary in order to enable it to carry out its functions.
Under this enablement, the Provisional Government (Transfer of
Functions) Order 1922 was made, which provided that all existing
laws, institutions, and authorities in Southern Ireland, whether
judicial, administrative, or ministerial, should continue, subject to the
necessary modifications therein contained. This had the effect of
transferring the control of the judicial system to the provisional
government, but before considering how this power was exercised,
it is necessary to examine what had happened to the courts in
Southern Ireland since the 1920 Act had been brought into force.

The Dáil Courts

Part of the programme of the revolutionary Dáil during the period
1919–1921 involved the establishment of a system of 'courts',
designed to give colour to the theory of *de jure* sovereignty and
(more important) to administer justice in those areas that the insurrectionary movement had deprived of the service of the ordinary
courts. A decree of the republican government, dated 29 June 1920,
established 'courts of justice and equity' and also empowered the
(republican) Ministry of Home Affairs to set up courts with criminal
jurisdiction.

By September 1920, the following judicial structure had been
created: (a) 'Parish Courts', consisting of three members, meeting
once a week and dealing with small civil and criminal cases, (b)
'District Courts', comprising five members, meeting once a month,
and dealing with more important civil and criminal cases, or cases
which came before them on appeal from the Parish Courts. In
addition, there were three sessions during the year in which a
circuit judge presided over the District Court, which then became
a 'Circuit Court', with unlimited civil and criminal jurisdiction.
There were four circuit judges and four circuit districts. (c) A
'Supreme Court' in Dublin, composed of not less than three

members appointed for three years, functioning both as a court of first instance and as an appellate tribunal.

The legal system applicable in these courts was the law as it stood at 21 January 1919, save as amended by the Dáil. It was also provided that, though British legal works were not to be used in argument, "the early Irish law codes", decisions of continental courts, and Roman law could be cited as persuasive authorities. The attitude of the legal profession to these arrangements was cautious. The Incorporated Law Society of Ireland considered a resolution aimed at preventing solicitors from appearing before Parish and District Courts, but the resolution was dropped. The General Council of the Bar of Ireland passed a resolution declaring it to be unprofessional for counsel to appear before the republican courts; but a general meeting of the Bar decided to take no action against counsel who ignored the resolution.

The civil authorities in Ireland, faced with the existence of this extensive system of what were regarded by them as illegal courts, were also embarrassed by the fact that the courts professed to be nothing more than arbitration tribunals. Their suppression was decided on, however, on the ground that they were functioning under the authority of a treasonable organisation, the First Dáil, and that this rendered them seditious assemblies. In the south and west of the country, however, the Dáil courts managed to function fairly regularly, and there were said to be over nine hundred Parish Courts and over seventy District Courts in operation by July 1921.

When the provisional government took over the administration of what was to become, under the terms of the Treaty, the Irish Free State, it found itself in possession of two separate systems of courts: these Dáil Courts, operating under the decrees of the revolutionary cabinet, and the Supreme Court of Judicature in Southern Ireland, the County Courts, and the Courts of Petty Sessions, all of which had been transferred to the new administration. The government was thus faced with alternatives: it could either consolidate these Dáil Courts, or it could utilise the ordinary courts which had been handed over. The latter course was adopted. A decree of the 'cabinet of Dáil Éireann'—which was coextensive with the provisional government—abolished all the Dáil Courts, other than the District and Parish Courts, with effect from 25 July 1922. District and Parish Courts were abolished on 16 October 1922, by another decree, on the basis that "the former British Courts were now in Irish hands."

The ultimate fate of these tribunals is of interest. By the Dáil Éireann Courts (Winding-Up) Act 1923, the Parliament of the Irish Free State provided for the appointment of a commissioner with wide powers to settle questions arising out of the judgments of the former Dáil Courts. The policy of this Act seems to have been to save their judgments, but it made clear that any validity those judgments might have, was conferred, not recognised, by the Act. As far as the courts of the Irish Free State were concerned, the decrees of the Dáil Courts were regarded as being not only void, but also illegal; for there was no continuity, in law, between the courts of the revolution and those of the Irish Free State. [2]

The revolutionary Dáil had also established a 'Land Settlement Court' in 1920, aimed at carrying out resettlement policies with respect to agricultural land. In 1924 an amending statute to the Dáil Éireann Courts (Winding-Up) Act 1923 was passed, declaring that the decrees of this court were to be treated as arbitration awards which might be confirmed by the Irish Land Commission.

[2] R. (Kelly) v. Maguire and O'Sheil [1923] 2 I.R.58.

CHAPTER V

THE COURTS SINCE 1922

It has already been shown that when the Irish Free State acquired its legal existence, it took over the system of courts which had been set up under the Government of Ireland Act 1920 for the short-lived state of Southern Ireland. It remains to be seen what further changes were necessary in order to create the modern system of courts in the territory that was ultimately to become the Republic of Ireland.

As a first step, the provisional government was faced with the problem caused by the breakdown of the courts of Petty Sessions. The disturbed state of the country, the secession of many litigants to the Dáil Courts, coupled with the fact that many of the holders of the commission of the peace and of the existing Resident Magistrates were not acceptable to the new régime, created an emergency, for it was necessary that the administration of justice in the inferior courts should be carried on. As a result, the provisional government adopted the expedient of appointing certain persons, described as 'District Justices', under the provisions of the Constabulary (Ireland) Act 1836, which, it will be recalled, empowered the appointment of Resident Magistrates. This was effected by a decree of the Minister for Home Affairs dated 26 October 1922. Moreover, under the Adaptation of Enactments Act 1922, section 6, all powers of Justices of the Peace or of Resident Magistrates, conferred by any statute, were made exercisable by a District Justice.

Under the District Justices (Temporary Provisions) Act 1923, statutory authority was conferred on the Governor General of the Irish Free State, on the advice of the Executive Council, to appoint District Justices. In order to remove doubts, the names of those persons who had been appointed as 'magistrates' by the decree of

26 October 1922, were scheduled to the Act, their appointment was confirmed, and they were indemnified as to their actions from that date. These District Justices continued to function under this legislation until the District Court was set up in 1924.

The Court of Appeal, the High Court, the County Courts and the Recorders' Courts continued to function as before. The judges were retained in office without any formal reappointment, though, in general, casual vacancies were not filled.

Under the Consitution of the Irish Free State, which came into force on 6 December 1922, article 63 provided that the judicial power of the Free State should be exercised, and justice administered in public courts established by Parliament, by judges to be appointed by the Governor General on the advice of the Executive Council, who were not to be removed except "for stated misbehaviour or incapacity, and then only by resolutions passed by both Dáil Éireann and Seanad Éireann." These courts were to be "Courts of First Instance and a Court of Final Appeal, to be called the Supreme Court . . . The Courts of First Instance shall include a High Court . . . invested with full original jurisdiction in and power to determine all matters and questions whether of law or fact, civil or criminal, and also courts of local and limited jurisdiction, with a right of appeal as determined by law." The number of judges, the constitution and organisation of, and distribution of business and jurisdiction amongst, these courts and judges were to be prescribed by law.

Article 73 continued in force the laws at the date of the coming into operation of the Constitution, while article 75 provided that, pending the establishment of courts in accordance with the Constitution, the Supreme Court of Judicature, County Courts, Courts of Quarter Sessions and courts of summary jurisdiction should continue to exercise the same jurisdiction as before.

In order to implement these constitutional provisions, a judiciary committee was appointed on 27 January 1923 to advise the Executive Council as to the establishment of the new courts and their jurisdiction. The committee was requested to approach these problems "untrammelled by any regard to any of the existing systems of judicature" in the country, and the existing framework of law and justice was described as "a standing monument of alien government." These weighty matters were considered by the committee with commendable speed, for it was able to report on 25 May 1923, setting out the scheme which was to be enacted into law by the Courts of Justice Act 1924.

The policy underlying this scheme appears to have been a recasting of the system of courts with a view to decentralising the administration of justice, but there was very little change in the principles involved. The following was the basis of the new judicial system:

(i) Petty Sessions were abolished and replaced by a unified District Court, presided over by a paid District Justice. The Justice of the Peace disappeared, but a new functionary, called a 'Peace Commissioner', was created to discharge the non-judicial functions, such as signing summonses, formerly carried out by the Justices. The jurisdiction of the criminal side of the District Court was still, in substance, that of summary jurisdiction for minor offences, together with the duty of the preliminary investigation of indictable offences. The civil jurisdiction was increased to £25 in contract and £10 in tort.

(ii) County Courts were abolished, and, in their place, a 'Circuit Court of Justice' was set up. The state was divided into eight circuits, each under a circuit judge, and each representing about 400,000 people. The civil jurisdiction was to extend to £300 for debt or damages, with an equity jurisdiction up to £1,000. On the criminal side, the Court could try all felonies and misdemeanours except murder, treason and piracy. It heard appeals from the District Court. Appeals from the Circuit Court on the civil side went to the High Court, where they were heard by two judges on the basis of the written transcript of the proceedings in the lower Court. Criminal appeals went to the Court of Criminal Appeal mentioned below.

(iii) The High Court of Justice consisted of six judges, one of whom, the 'President of the High Court', presided. This Court corresponded to the old High Court of Justice in Southern Ireland and had all the jurisdiction of that court transferred to it. It also provided one of its number to preside at the 'Central Criminal Court' in Dublin, an extension of the old Dublin City Commission, where all serious crime from the country was to be tried.

(iv) The Supreme Court of Justice was composed of three judges, one of whom was the Chief Justice of the Irish Free State. It had all the appellate jurisdiction of the old Court of Appeal, together with that prescribed by the Constitution. The functions of the Lord

Chancellor in connection with wards of court, lunatics, and the discipline of solicitors were transferred to the Chief Justice.

(v) A Court of Criminal Appeal was established, consisting of three judges, one of whom was to be the Chief Justice or a judge of the Supreme Court, the others being members of the High Court; in special cases the Chief Justice could request additional judges of the Supreme Court or the High Court to sit. This Court corresponded to the Court of Criminal Appeal set up in England, under the Criminal Appeal Act 1907. Its decision was final, unless the Attorney General certified that the case involved a point of exceptional public importance, when a further appeal could be taken to the Supreme Court.

(vi) Provision was also made in the Act of 1924 for the setting up of a 'Court of the High Court Circuit', and it seems to have been contemplated that a tribunal similar to the old Court of Assize would travel through the country for the purpose of hearing criminal cases within the jurisdiction of the High Court. This was to supplement the Central Criminal Court in Dublin. This plan was never put into operation and the provisions were repealed in 1926.

These courts, set up under the Courts of Justice Act 1924, continued to operate in the Irish Free State until that political entity ceased to exist in 1937. There were some minor changes but the main framework remained unchanged. A joint committee of both Houses of the Oireachtas, set up to consider the working of the new courts, reported in 1930 and, as a result, certain alterations were made. The strength of the Supreme Court was increased to five judges; the system of appeals from the Circuit Court was abolished and replaced by an appeal to a judge of the High Court, travelling on circuit, by way of rehearing; the jurisdiction of the Chief Justice over wards of court and lunatics was transferred to the President of the High Court; and certain other minor amendments were made. [1] Earlier, the Court of Criminal Appeal had been empowered to direct a retrial in certain cases, a power not possessed by the corresponding court in England. [2]

On 29 December 1937, the Constitution of Ireland came into operation, supplanting the earlier instrument of 1922. Article 34 made provision for the administration of justice "in public courts

[1] Courts of Justice Act 1936.
[2] Courts of Justice Act 1928.

established by law by judges appointed in the manner provided by this Constitution", and these courts were to include "Courts of First Instance and a Court of Final Appeal." The Courts of First Instance were to consist of a High Court, and also "courts of local and limited jurisdiction", while the Court of Final Appeal was to be called the Supreme Court.

These constitutional provisions contemplated the establishment of courts by the Oireachtas or National Parliament, for by article 58, the existing courts and judges were to continue to exercise the same jurisdiction as theretofore, "until otherwise determined by law." No such determination was made until 1961, though attention was drawn to the anomalous situation thus created. [3]

The matter was then dealt with by legislation, under the Courts (Establishment and Constitution) Act 1961 and the Courts (Supplemental Provisions) Act 1961. The first of these statutes establishes formally, in accordance with Article 34 of the Constitution, the Supreme Court, the High Court, the Court of Criminal Appeal, the Circuit Court, and the District Court. It then proceeds to disestablish the existing courts, which had continued to function under article 58 of the Constitution, and to abolish the offices of existing judges and justices.

The second statute provides for the several matters specified in article 36 of the Constitution as matters to be "regulated in accordance with law": the number of judges and their remuneration, age of retirement and pensions, the organisation of the courts, the arrangement of jurisdiction, and all matters of procedure. This is done very largely by reference to existing enactments, but the opportunity has been taken to consolidate some of the statutory material relating to jurisdiction.

Under the second statute, the existing judges and justices were eligible for appointment to corresponding judicial offices in the courts established in the first statute, and it was provided that if they were willing to accept office, no other person would be qualified for appointment as the first judges and justices of the newly established courts.

It now remains for us to examine in more detail the jurisdiction conferred on the several courts in criminal matters and civil matters, and to see how that jurisdiction is exercised.

[3] *The State (Killian)* v. *Minister for Justice* [1954] I.R. 207.

CHAPTER VI

THE CRIMINAL JURISDICTION OF THE COURTS

Original Criminal Jurisdiction

It has already been shown that the earliest function of the King's Courts in England was the business of trying serious criminal offences at Assize. This was based on the theory that the wrongdoer was entitled to a trial by a jury of his fellow-countrymen, drawn from the locality in which he resided or in which the crime had been committed. At first, indeed, the investigation and punishment of all kinds of crime occupied the time of the judge of Assize, but after the creation of the office of Justice of the Peace in the fourteenth century, much of the work in connection with the less serious type of offence was passed over to the justices.

Quarter Sessions were held four times a year for the purpose of trying criminal offences, with the proviso that difficult cases should be reserved to the judge of Assize. No definite provision was made for the trial of what would now be called 'summary offences', but, gradually, a series of statutes created petty offences which were triable by the justices out of sessions. In addition, the justices acquired the power to hold preliminary investigations into allegations of crimes which might result in trials at Quarter Sessions or at Assizes. These investigations were in the nature of police inquiries, at a time when there was no organised police force. The expression "summary jurisdiction", then, came to mean the power of justices to hear and determine a criminal charge in a summary way, without the intervention of a jury. This was entirely the creation of statute, for the justices had no common law power to try offences in this way.

This development has been mirrored in the history of the courts in Ireland, where similar powers devolved on the Justices of the

Peace, the Resident Magistrates, and ultimately, on the District Justices. Moreover, the Constitution of 1937, which guarantees trial by jury, continues to recognise the right of summary trial of minor offences.

At the beginning of the nineteenth century, the situation in Ireland was that a person accused of a crime was brought before the justices, frequently at their private residences. If a minor offence was alleged, then the case was disposed of summarily. There were hardly any rules of procedure. If the case was about a more serious offence, the justices would proceed to hear the evidence for the prosecution in order to determine whether there was a prima facie case against the accused. If such a case was made out, the accused would be 'returned for trial' at the next Assizes or Quarter Sessions. By convention, Quarter Sessions did not try offences carrying the death penalty, which at that time meant that a large number of cases were excluded from them and had to be tried at Assize.

In either case, the procedure was the same. A Grand Jury was summoned. This jury was 'charged' or addressed by the judge on the 'state of the county', and then 'bills of indictment', or formal written accusations were put before it. The Grand Jury, sitting in secret, heard as much of the evidence for the prosecution as it wished to hear, and then decided whether the accused ought to be tried or not. Although most bills of indictment related to persons who were returned for trial by the justices, anyone could put forward an accusation of this type. In eighteenth-century Ireland, indeed, it was not customary for the Crown to prosecute at Assizes except for some pressing reason, and the prosecution of crime was left in the hands of the private prosecutor.

This practice changed in 1801, when Crown Solicitors responsible for Crown prosecutions were appointed for each of the circuits. About 1830, moreover, the Attorney General began to direct a solicitor in each county, who was called a 'Sessional Crown Solicitor', to conduct prosecutions at Quarter Sessions and, sometimes, at Petty Sessions as well, though many of the summary cases were conducted by police officers. At the end of the nineteenth century the offices of Crown Solicitor (for Assizes) and Sessional Crown Solicitor were being amalgamated, and this process was complete by 1914. In 1922 these officials were replaced by an equivalent called the 'State Solicitor.'

The Courts of Justice Act 1924 abolished the Grand Jury, and the Criminal Justice (Administration) Act 1924 provided that all criminal charges prosecuted upon indictment should be conducted at the suit of the Attorney General. It is now settled that the whole basis of the jurisdiction to try a criminal charge on indictment is the preliminary examination conducted by a district justice in accordance with the rules of procedure governing such examination. The right of the private prosecutor to prefer a bill of indictment is abolished. [1] He can institute proceedings in the District Court, but if the accused is sent forward for trial, the Attorney General then takes charge. [2]

Under the Prosecution of Offences Act 1974, most of the functions of the Attorney General in relation to criminal matters have been transferred to a newly-created officer called the Director of Public Prosecutions (the DPP) created by that Act. The DPP, who is appointed by the government, will be independent in the performance of his functions. To this end, he is afforded guarantees against arbitrary dismissal. This new office has been created so as to remove the decision to institute prosecutions from any appearance or suspicion of amenability to political pressure. Indeed, the Act makes it unlawful to try to influence such a decision. The creation of a DPP, which is generally agreed to be long overdue, will have the incidental advantage of enabling the Attorney General to devote himself more fully to giving general legal advice to the government – an increasingly onerous task in the wake of Ireland's accession to the European Communities. However, in criminal cases, where the constitutional validity of a law is called in question, the Attorney General will retain his former functions. His consent must still be obtained for prosecutions under the Geneva Conventions Act 1962, the Official Secrets Act 1963 and the Genocide Act 1973. And at any time, the government, in the interests of national security, may transfer the functions of the DPP in relation to specified crimes back to the Attorney General.

The following courts exercise original criminal jurisdiction in the Republic of Ireland at the present time:

[1] *The People (Attorney General)* v. *Boggan* (1958) I.R. 67.
[2] *The People* v. *Killeen* (1958) I.L.T.R. 182.

1. *The District Court*

In the District Court, the district justice sits without a jury. The Court's competence is therefore restricted by the Constitution, Article 38.5 of which provides that, except in the case of minor offences, military offences tried by court martial, and in emergency circumstances, no person is to be tried on any criminal charge without a jury.

The criminal jurisdiction of the District Court falls under the following heads:

(i) Minor offences created by statute and stated to be triable in a summary way. These include most road traffic offences, whose disposal makes up a large portion of the criminal work of this court. The primary consideration in determining whether an offence is minor, and so constitutionally triable before the District Court, is the punishment it may attract. [3] In one case the Supreme Court decided that the existence of a penalty of three years detention took the offence out of this category. [4] Generally the maximum penalty for offences triable summarily does not exceed six months imprisonment or a fine of £100. However, under some statutes the Court has power to impose swingeing penalties of other sorts. It may disqualify a person convicted of drunken driving for up to three years [5] and, under the Fisheries (Consolidation) Act 1959, it may order the forfeiture of the fish and fishing gear found on board a foreign fishing boat illegally fishing within the fishery limits of the state.

(ii) Indictable offences specified in the schedule of the Criminal Justice Act 1951 as amended, if

(a) the Court is of opinion that the facts proved or alleged constitute a minor offence, and

(b) the accused, on being informed by the Court of his right to be tried with a jury, does not object to being tried summarily.

Offences triable summarily in this way include perjury, forgery, certain forms of assult, and larceny involving property the value of which does not exceed £200. In the case of some such offences, e.g.

---

[3] See *Melling* v. *O'Mathghamhna and the Attorney General* [1962] I.R. 1; *Conroy* v. *Attorney General and Another* [1965] I.R. 411.

[4] *The State (Sheerin)* v. *Kennedy and Others* [1966] I.R. 379.

[5] Road Traffic Act 1961, Section 49.

perjury and larceny, the consent of the Director of Public Prosecutions is also required for a summary trial.

(iii) Indictable offences (other than murder, treason, piracy and grave breaches of the Geneva Conventions on War Crimes) where the accused, when before the District Court, wishes to plead guilty, and the District Justice is satisfied that he understands the charge. Under Section 13 of the Criminal Procedure Act 1967, the Court may deal summarily with such a case if the Director of Public Prosecutions does not object. Otherwise, the accused must be sent forward to the Circuit Court or the Central Criminal Court for sentence. [6] In that event, he may alter his plea to not guilty. If the District Court deals with the case, the maximum punishment it may impose is a fine of £100 and imprisonment for twelve months. The Committee on Court Practice and Procedure, in its Fifth Interim Report published in 1966, recommended that this limitation should be removed. The fact that a trial is avoided by a plea of guilty in the District Court should not, argued the Committee, afford to the offender an assurance of a sentence in the District Court no greater than that which would be appropriate to a minor offence only. There was a danger that pleas of guilty might be induced by the expectation of lower sentences. But deterred, perhaps, by constitutional objections to an extension of the District Court's jurisdiction, successive governments have taken no action to extend its sentencing powers in accordance with this recommendation.

(iv) Indictable offences not triable summarily. In such cases, unless the accused waives it, there is a preliminary examination by the District Court at which the prosecution must disclose the evidence against the accused. The District Justice considers this and any material submitted on behalf of the accused. If he thinks that there is a sufficient case to put the accused on trial, he sends him forward to the Circuit Court or the Central Criminal Court. Otherwise he discharges him. The reasons for this preliminary examination are to ensure that an accused is not put on trial for a serious offence merely upon accusation, and to give him advance notice of the case he will have to answer at the actual trial. It should be noted that by virtue of Section 62 of the Courts of Justice Act 1936, the Director of Public Prosecutions is empowered, in certain circumstances, to

[6] See *The State (John Williams)* v. *Kelly* (No. 2) [1970] I.R. 271.

direct that a person charged with an indictable offence should be sent forward for trial despite the fact that the District Justice before whom he is charged has discharged him. This power, which is intended to be used to rectify errors of principle, is sparingly exercised.

(v) Crimes committed by children under sixteen. A Justice of the the District Court may sit as 'The Children's Court' and deal in such manner as shall seem just with all charges against children, except those whose gravity makes them unfit to be so dealt with.

2. The Circuit Court

The original criminal jurisdiction of the Circuit Court is confined to indictable offences. Under Section 25 of the Courts (Supplemental Provisions) Act 1961, it may try any offence on indictment except treason, murder, attempt or conspiracy to murder, piracy, and certain serious offences under the Treason Act 1939 and the Offences against the State Act 1939. This jurisdiction is exercisable by the judge (sitting with a jury) of the circuit in which the offence has been committed or in which the accused person has been arrested or resides. The judge may transfer a criminal trial from one part of his circuit to another. On the application of either the Director of Public Prosecutions or the accused, he is obliged to transfer the case to the Central Criminal Court. The prime purpose of these provisions is to enable parties in a country case to avoid trial before a local jury. However, there has been a resulting tendency to overload the Central Criminal Court with relatively minor criminal cases, especially since a former restriction, limiting this power of transfer to cases involving a maximum penalty of more than one year's imprisonment or five years' penal servitude, was repealed by Section 6 of the Courts Act 1964. The Committee on Court Practice and Procedure, in its Sixth Interim Report published in 1966, suggested that the circuit courts outside Dublin should only be entitled to transfer to the Central Criminal Court cases involving points of constitutional law or requiring adjudication upon the validity of the return for trial from the District Court. No action has been taken on this recommendation, perhaps because it may not be constitutionally proper to exclude the trial of any major criminal offence from the High Court, invested as it is with full original jurisdiction to determine all matters and questions whether of law or fact, civil or criminal.

3. *The Central Criminal Court*

The High Court exercising the criminal jurisdiction with which it is invested is known as the Central Criminal Court. This Court has power to sit anywhere in the state but, in practice, its sittings are held in Dublin at Green Street Courthouse, where it combines the old jurisdiction of the Dublin City Commission with that of the Courts of Assize. The original criminal jurisdiction to try crime on indictment is exercised by a judge or judges of the High Court (sitting with a jury) nominated by the President of the High Court. Normally the function is exercised by each judge so nominated, but the President has power to direct two or more judges to sit together for the purpose of a particular case.

4. *Special Criminal Courts*

When the government is satisfied that the ordinary courts are inadequate to secure the effective administration of justice and the preservation of public peace and order, it is empowered, under Part V of the Offences against the State Act 1939, to establish a Special Criminal Court to try specified offences scheduled by government order and also other cases where the DPP so requests. This court must consist of three persons; it sits without a jury and delivers only one decision. Special criminal courts have been established in 1939, in 1961, and most recently in 1970. On former occasions army officers were appointed but, since 1970, the court has consisted entirely of members of the judiciary, including district justices and a retired judge. While the Offences against the State Act 1939 provides that the Special Criminal Court is to follow, as far as practicable, the procedures and rules of evidence applicable in the Central Criminal Court, a serious exception was created by an amending Act passed in November 1972, which provided that a statement by an officer of the Garda Síochána, not below the rank of Chief Superintendant, that he believes the accused to be a member of an illegal organisation, was to be evidence of that fact.

Appellate Criminal Jurisdiction

1. *The Circuit Court*

An appeal lies from a decision of the District Court in order to challenge the order of the lower court on its merits. The appeal takes the form of a rehearing of the whole case, and either party has the right to call fresh evidence other than that given in the District Court. The appeal is on the merits, however, and if an allegation is made that the order of the District Justice is defective as to form, the proper remedy is not an appeal to the Circuit Court, but an application to the High Court for a prerogative order of *Certiorari*.

Normally, the right to appeal against a decision of the District Court is confined to the accused person, but there are a number of statutes which confer a right of appeal on the complainant as well. [7] The Circuit Court (which in this case sits without a jury) may confirm, vary or reverse the order of the District Justice, but it has not got the power to quash the order on the basis that it is bad *in form*, as being in excess of jurisdiction. The decision of the Circuit Court on appeal is final, conclusive and not appealable.

2. *The High Court*

(i) As successor to the old Court of King's Bench, the High Court is vested with an inherent jurisdiction in connection with what used to be called the 'Prerogative Writs.' These are now orders which are granted by the High Court and are directed to any inferior tribunal for the purpose of bringing up the orders or decisions of that inferior tribunal for review. They are not concerned with the merits of the orders of the inferior tribunals, but are directed to ascertaining whether the jurisdiction has been exceeded. The prerogative orders are those of *Certiorari*, *Mandamus*, and *Prohibition*.

Certiorari lies to challenge an order which is made in excess of jurisdiction; which disregards the essentials of justice; which is obtained by fraud; or where there is bias in the tribunal whose order is sought to be impugned. *Mandamus* is an order issuing from the High Court directed to any person or inferior court, requiring him or them to do some particular thing, or to perform a legal duty. *Prohibition* will issue from the High Court to restrain an inferior court from usurping a jurisdiction, or from acting in excess of its statutory power.

These applications are made to the High Court in the form of an application for a conditional order to show cause why they should

---

[7] The right of appeal is generally conferred by old statutes carried over under the Criminal Justice Act 1928, section 18. A more modern example is the Fisheries (Consolidation) Act 1959.

not be granted. The justice against whom the conditional order is made then comes before the High Court and seeks to show why the order should not be made.

(ii) In addition to reviewing the decisions of inferior tribunals by the prerogative orders, the High Court has jurisdiction to give a ruling on a question of law submitted to it by the District Court. [8] This is known as procedure by way of 'case stated.' In the District Court, a district justice may, either before or after he decides a cause before him, and either of his own volition or on application of one of the parties thereto, state a case on a question of law for the consideration of the High Court. Even if the justice should refuse to state a case on the application of one of the parties, that party may apply to the High Court for an order directed to the justice obliging him to do so. The decisions of the High Court may take the form of answers to the questions submitted to it, with a remission of the case to the District Court, or it may take the form of a reversal, affirmation, or amendment of the decision in the court below.

3. *The Court of Criminal Appeal*

This Court, which was first established in Ireland under the Courts of Justice Act 1924, exists for the purpose of hearing appeals by convicted persons in cases tried on indictment in the Central Criminal Court and in the Circuit Court. The Court of Criminal Appeal is comprised of three judges, one of whom is the Chief Justice or a judge of the Supreme Court nominated by him, and the other two judges of the High Court. The determination of questions before the Court is that of the majority of its members, and only one judgment is pronounced.

A person convicted on indictment before either the Central Criminal Court, the Circuit Court or the Special Criminal Court, may appeal to the Court of Criminal Appeal, provided that he obtains a certificate from the trial judge that the case is suitable for appeal, or, in the case of refusal, provided that the Court of Criminal Appeal itself grants such leave to appeal. The grant of a certificate by the trial judge is a rare occurrence. Thus the usual case that comes before the Court is one in which the applicant is seeking leave to appeal. Such leave is granted where the Court is of opinion that a question of law is involved, or where the trial appears

[8] Courts (Supplemental Provisions) Act 1961, Section 52.

to have been unsatisfactory, and the Court has power to affirm the conviction, reverse it in whole or in part, and reduce or increase the sentence. Where the Court reverses a conviction as a whole, it has, in addition, power to order that the accused be retried for the same offence. Moreover, the Court, notwithstanding that it is of opinion that a point raised in the appeal might be decided in favour of the accused, may dismiss the appeal if it considers that no miscarriage of justice has actually occurred.

The Committee on Court Practice and Procedure, in its Seventh Interim Report published in 1966, considered the question of appeals from convictions on indictment. They recommended that the Court of Criminal Appeal should be abolished and its functions transferred to the Supreme Court. The reasons were part administrative and part constitutional. The changing composition of the Court of Criminal Appeal deprived it of the element of continuity. Its sittings interfered with those of the High and Supreme Courts from which its members were drawn. It was anomalous, in the Committee's view, that High Court judges should sit on appeal from the judgments of other High Court judges. Under the Constitution, an appellant wishing to question the constitutional validity of a law could take that point only in the Supreme Court. Accordingly, he could be involved in a multiplicity of appeal procedures on different issues in one case. The Committee recommended that the Supreme Court should be the only court of appeal from convictions on indictment. On such appeals, each member of the Supreme Court should be free to give a separate opinion, except that, on sentence, only one opinion should be pronounced. The unreal distinction between an application for leave to appeal and an actual appeal should be abolished, and every convicted person should have the right to appeal without the preliminary requirement of obtaining a certificate from the trial judge (which is rarely given) or leave to appeal from the court hearing the appeal. No action was taken on these recommendations in the Criminal Procedure Act 1967 or in subsequent legislation.

4. *The Supreme Court*

(i) By virtue of Section 29 of the Courts of Justice Act 1924, the accused may appeal from the Court of Criminal Appeal to the Supreme Court, if the Attorney General or the Court of Criminal

Appeal itself certifies that the decision involves a point of law of exceptional public importance and that it is desirable in the public interest that the opinion of the Supreme Court be taken thereon.

(ii) An appeal lies directly from the Central Criminal Court to the Supreme Court against interlocutory orders, e.g. in regard to bail pending trial, or awards of cost. The Committee on Court Practice and Procedure, in its Seventh Interim Report, adverted to the possibility that the right of appeal to the Court of Criminal Appeal against conviction in the Central Criminal Court may not, as a matter of law, exclude a direct appeal to the Supreme Court in such cases.

(iii) Where, on a question of law, a verdict in favour of an accused person is found by direction of the judge in a trial on indictment, the Attorney General may refer that question of law to the Supreme Court for determination. The acquittal of the accused stands, notwithstanding the outcome of such a reference. [9]

(iv) Under Section 16 of the Courts of Justice Act 1947, a Circuit Court judge may, on the application of any party to any matter before him, refer any question of law arising to the Supreme Court by way of a 'case stated.' This procedure is little used in criminal trials before juries because of the necessity to adjourn the trial pending the Supreme Court's determination.

(v) An appeal lies to the Supreme Court from the grant or refusal by the High Court of an order for habeas corpus. [10]

(vi) Where a prerogative order is obtained in the High Court, directed to the District Court, or if such order is refused, an appeal against the decision of the High Court lies to the Supreme Court.

(vii) Either the prosecution or the accused can appeal to the Supreme Court from the High Court on a 'case stated' from the District Court, provided that they obtain leave from the High Court to do so. The Committee on Court Practice and Procedure, in its Eleventh Interim Report published in 1970, recommended that there should be an appeal against refusal of such leave to appeal, since important points of law may arise which merit consideration by the Supreme Court.

---

[9] Criminal Procedure Act 1967, Section 34.
[10] *The State* (*Browne*) v. *Feran* [1967] I.R. 147.

Criminal Procedure

In cases involving the summary jurisdiction, proceedings are initiated by the making of a 'complaint' or the laying of an 'information.' This complaint or information is made to the justice, to a peace commissioner, or to the justice's clerk, and is followed by the issue of a District Court summons. This summons sets out briefly the cause of the complaint, and calls upon the defendant to attend the Court to answer it. It must be served on the defendant in one of the ways prescribed in the rules of the District Court. The justice has also got power in certain cases to order the arrest of the defendant in the first instance, or in default of his appearance to a summons.

When the case comes on for hearing, the justice hears the evidence adduced by the complainant and the defendant, listens to such legal submissions as may be made to him by the advisers to either party, and then gives his decision, which is incorporated in the order set out by him in his minute book. It is this record in the minute book that forms the basis of his order.

Prosecutions for indictable offences may also be commenced by summons or warrant for arrest, in order to procure the attendance of the person charged. The general rule is that a warrant ought not to be issued in the first instance, unless the offence is of a serious nature. When the accused appears before the District Court, a preliminary examination takes place. The accused is served with a statement of the charge and of the evidence intended to be adduced, and also a list of witnesses and exhibits. At the hearing, either side may require any witness to be called and his evidence taken down in writing, read over, and signed by him. This sworn transcript of evidence is called a deposition. Witnesses called by one side may be cross-examined by the other. Finally, the accused, on being cautioned, may make a statement which is taken down in writing and may be used in evidence at his trial.

If, having heard submissions on both sides, the justice is of opinion that the evidence is sufficient to put the accused on trial, he sends him forward for trial either in custody or on bail. In most serious cases, the justice decides whether bail will be granted or not; in granting bail, he is required to exercise his discretion in accordance with well-settled principles. A refusal of bail may result in an application being made to the High Court to admit the accused to bail.

When the accused has been returned for trial, the prosecution prepares the indictment, which is, in effect, a written statement of the offence or offences with which he is charged. He is then arraigned before the judge of the Circuit Court or the Central Criminal Court, a jury is empanelled, and he 'pleads' to the indictment, i.e. he states whether he is guilty or not guilty of the crime charged. The trial then proceeds with an opening statement by counsel for the prosecution, the calling of the prosecution witnesses, examination and cross-examination, followed by the hearing of the case for the defence in the same way. The accused may or may not elect to give evidence on his own behalf; if he refuses, his failure to do so must not be the subject of comment by the prosecution, though the trial judge is not inhibited in this way. Counsel on each side then sum up, the judge directs the jury on the law and reviews the evidence, and the jury retire to consider their verdict. They are required to be unanimous in their verdict. If they are unable to reach agreement, they are discharged and the accused is remanded, in custody or on bail, for retrial.

Courts Exercising Criminal Jurisdiction

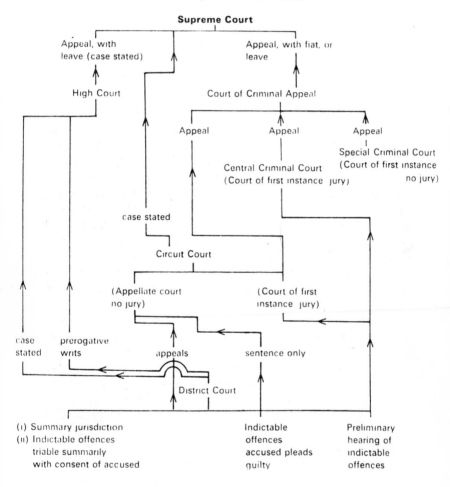

CHAPTER VII

THE CIVIL JURISDICTION OF THE COURTS

Civil Procedure

Ever since the Judicature (Ir.) Act 1877, most matters of practice and procedure connected with the conduct of civil actions in the High Court have been governed by Rules of Court. Under that statute, a Rules Committee was established which drew up regulations for the control of judicial proceedings in that Court. The last general revision of these rules was in 1962. The Supreme Court Rules Committee, consisting of eleven members drawn from the judiciary, the Bar and the solicitors' profession, is now charged with responsibility for revising the Rules of Court. The last general revision was effected in 1962. These rules are extremely complicated: they lay down with great particularity the steps to be followed in bringing actions in the High Court, and regulate all other matters connected with the working of the Court.

It would be inappropriate in a work of this compass to set out in detail the nature of the rules of court, but it should be pointed out that the expression 'practice and procedure' covers all the stages in the conduct of an action down to and including the trial and it also deals with matters affecting the enforcement of judgments and the bringing of appeals to the Supreme Court. In this connection, too, it must be remembered that only a very small proportion of actions begun in the courts ever come to trial at all. Many of them are settled by agreement between the parties, or the defendant submits to judgment on the basis that he has no defence. In many cases, also, the issue of a summons is only a tactic designed to stimulate a settlement. Thus, in the common case of an action arising out of personal injuries sustained by a pedestrian in a motor accident, where the defendant motorist is represented by an insurance company, the pedestrian's legal advisers will try to settle the case by obtaining payment from the insurers. If they fail, then a summons will be issued and the plaintiff will indicate his willingness to pursue the claim. In such a case, it is common for the defendant to pay into court a sum which he considers sufficient to satisfy the claim. In such a case, the plaintiff is faced with the decision as to whether he will take the amount tendered and discontinue proceedings, or will go ahead with his action. If he chooses the latter course, he is confronted with a further problem: should he obtain more damages than the amount lodged in court, he will get his costs in the ordinary way, but if he does not, then he must pay his own costs and the costs of the defendant after the date of the lodgment in court.

There are certain types of proceedings in the High Court which are designed to deal with actions which are unlikely to be contested. If, for instance, the defendant ignores the proceedings and does not enter an 'appearance', provision is made in the rules for obtaining summary judgment; there is a similar procedure where the plaintiff makes an affidavit to the effect that he believes there is no defence to his claim. The great majority of actions, then, are compromised or settled in some way before trial.

Pleadings

In English law, there has always been a fundamental difference between the system of trial used in the Courts of Common Law and that used in the Court of Chancery. In the old Common Law Courts—the Queen's Bench, the Exchequer and the Common Pleas— the introduction of a system of trial by jury at an early stage meant that the court was inclined to treat each party as being on an equal footing, and not to afford the plaintiff any assistance in prosecuting his claim. It was up to the plaintiff to select the appropriate writ, and to ensure that the case was made ready for hearing. The only function of the judge was to act as a sort of umpire and to take the verdict of the jury. In the Court of Chancery, on the other hand, the procedure was more in the nature of an inquisition. The Chancellor thought that it was part of his duty to get to the bottom of the issue in dispute, and he evolved a system of oral or written interrogatories by which he was enabled to extract the truth from the defendant. He could also compel either party to produce any documents in their possession relevant to the case.

Although the judge regarded himself as being an umpire in a common law action, nevertheless it was important for the dispute between the parties to be reduced to an agreed issue of facts. If this were not done, the inquiry might range over a field so wide that a jury would be incapable of understanding the questions involved and of giving a verdict. As a result, the system of 'pleadings' was evolved which is still operative in the High Court.

Originally, when a plaintiff issued a writ claiming relief from the defendant, the latter was at liberty to come to court and defend the case. It then became necessary for the judge to settle on some single question of fact which the jury could decide. This question was determined orally, after argument between the parties, and eventually a plea, or a series of pleas, was enrolled and tried. The defendant could 'traverse' the plaintiff's claim, i.e. deny it; he could 'demur' to it, i.e. state that even if the claim were true, it did not disclose a cause of action; or he could plead by way of 'confession and avoidance', i.e. admit the truth of the facts alleged against him, but introduce new facts which would entitle him to succeed.

With the passage of time, this system of oral pleading gave way to written pleadings, in which the allegations made by the parties were set out on paper. This meant that the science of pleading became much more exact and much more complicated, for an inadvertent slip was not easily rectified. By the beginning of the nineteenth century the whole affair had become extremely complex. Each writ, or 'form of action', had its own appropriate system of pleading, and the whole system had become highly specialised, so much so that it resulted in the development of a district branch of the legal profession, the 'special pleader'.

The reforms carried out in the practice and procedure of the courts in the nineteenth century, both in England and Ireland, abolished the old system of pleading, and substituted one single form of writ in which the cause of action could be simply stated. In addition, the Common Law Procedure (Ir.) Acts 1853–1856 provided for the application of many of the equitable remedies to the common law courts, and this tended to reduce the multiplicity of suits and to simplify legal proceedings generally. The Judicature (Ir.) Act 1877, in abolishing the old courts, assimilated the practice and procedure of these courts into one system in so far as it was possible to do so. The Courts of Justice Act 1924, and the rules made thereunder, changed the names of some of the forms of procedure prescribed under the old Judicature Act system, but left the main structure unchanged. Unskilful pleading may still delay an action at law, but will not often be fatal to the result.

The Conduct of an Action Today

In practice, most of the steps taken by a plaintiff in the conduct of an action are carried out by his solicitor in consultation with counsel, but for the purposes of the present discussion it will be assumed that the plaintiff is acting in person. Assuming that the action is one involving contested issues of fact, the first step is for the plaintiff to issue and serve on the defendant a 'Plenary Summons', which is the modern equivalent of the writ. The Plenary Summons has on it a 'General Indorsement of Claim,' which sets out as succinctly as possible the relief claimed and the grounds on which it is claimed. After the summons has been issued and served, the defendant enters a formal appearance in the appropriate office of the High Court. The plaintiff then sends to the defendant a document called a 'Statement of Claim' setting out in detail the allegations that he is making. This is responded to by the defendant sending a 'Defence' in which each allegation in the statement of claim is denied or otherwise dealt with. To this, in turn, the plaintiff may send a 'Reply', dealing with the matters raised in the defence.

None of these documents deals with the evidence with which the allegations are to be supported; they are merely designed to ensure that each party should know with reasonable particularity the case he will have to meet in court. The whole process of pleading is under the control of the court, through the agency of an officer called the 'Master of the High Court', with an appeal to a judge. Thus, it is possible for either party to obtain further and better particulars of any matter contained in a pleading, provided that these particulars are not a question of evidence; in the same way, it is possible to administer interrogatories to a party, or direct him to produce documents.

Under the rules of court, provision is made for the 'special indorsement' of a claim on a summons, called a 'Summary Summons', in cases which are, broadly speaking, simple claims for money due. This absolves the plaintiff from delivering a further statement of claim by putting his claim on the summons itself;

the defendant is then compelled to make his answer without further ado.

When all these steps have been completed, the pleadings are closed and the case is ready for trial. In the course of the preliminary operations, the place and mode of trial will have been settled. Under the rules of court, all High Court proceedings take place in Dublin, unless the Court otherwise orders. In practice, original proceedings are to an increasing extent being heard at other venues, by the judges of the High Court, when the High Court on Circuit is travelling through the country to hear appeals from the Circuit Court.

When a case comes to hearing, a choice must be made between trial before a judge alone and trial before a judge and jury. The question sometimes arises whether a party is entitled to a jury on the hearing of a plenary summons. Generally speaking, juries are allowed in all cases other than Chancery proceedings, actions for liquidated damages, actions for the enforcement of, or for breaches of, contract, and actions for the recovery of land. Chancery proceedings include matters formerly disposed of in the Chancery Division, such as the enforcement of trusts, the administration of the estates of deceased persons, the rectification of deeds, and applications for injunctions or specific performance. The vast majority of jury actions in the High Court are claims arising from personal injury or death caused by negligence or breach of statutory duty in road traffic or factory accidents. Probate actions, matrimonial causes or matters, actions for libel, slander, seduction, criminal conversation, false imprisonment and malicious prosecution are also generally tried in this way. Formerly there was a similar right to trial by jury in the Circuit Court but it was seldom exercised and eventually was abolished by the Courts Act 1971. In trials before a jury, questions of law are decided by the judge and questions of fact by the jury. In the old days there was a distinction between 'special juries' and 'common juries'. A special jury was drawn from more affluent people than a common jury on the theory that richer people were likely to be more intelligent. If a party applied for a special jury, he had to pay the cost of it unless the judge certified that it was a proper case for a special jury. Special juries have now been abolished. Moreover, since 1924, in civil cases, the majority vote of nine of the twelve jurors sworn is sufficient to determine the verdict.

The widespread availability of trial by jury has given rise to some controversy. In England and Wales, but not in Scotland and Northern Ireland, it is only available as of right in cases of libel, slander, malicious prosecution, false imprisonment, seduction and fraud. Even in these actions, it may be denied where the trial requires a prolonged examination of documents or accounts, or any scientific or local investigation. As a result of several decisions of the English Court of Appeal in the nineteen sixties, jury trial has been eliminated in negligence actions for personal injuries and death, except in very special circumstances. The Committee on Court Practice and Procedure, in its Third Interim Report published in 1965, considered the availability of jury trial in Ireland. By a majority, they recommended that the existing right to jury trial in civil actions in the High Court should be retained, subject to the right of the Court, on the application of either party, to order a trial without a jury where a case required a prolonged examination of documents or accounts or difficult scientific investigation. In support of this recommendation, they pointed to the superiority of a multi-member tribunal as a judge of fact, the importance of keeping the standards of the law from becoming remote from what the ordinary man desires, and the value of the diversity of experience that jurymen bring to the decision of a case. A substantial minority of the Committee were not so convinced, especially in relation to personal injury negligence cases. Juries, they maintained, were unduly sympathetic to plaintiffs in such cases since they knew that most defendants were insured. Also judgment on questions of fact often involved complicated inferences and this skilled task was best performed by trained persons. This minority also felt that jury verdicts were unpredictable, which increased the number of cases going to trial, and it was more difficult to review them on appeal since no reasons were given for decisions.

It should be noted that many of the matters dealt with on the Chancery side of the High Court do not involve contests at all. It often happens, for example, that trustees are in doubt as to their powers, and, before exercising them, they seek the advice and protection of the courts. Although there is no longer any 'Chancery Division' in the old sense, as a matter of practice all

Chancery work is assigned to two judges, popularly known as the 'Chancery Judges'.

The Judgment and its Enforcement

It has already been indicated that there are certain classes of case in which a plaintiff can obtain judgment 'in default'. These are cases in which the defendant either does not enter an appearance or a defence. Since 1926, the number of cases in which a judgment can be entered 'in default of defence' is more limited, and now only extends to actions brought on a plenary summons for a debt, for the recovery of land, or for the recovery of specific goods. In all other cases where no defence is delivered, application must be made to a judge for judgment, or to the Master. In addition, a defendant may have a default judgment set aside on the ground of fraud, mistake, surprise, or irregularity.

The great majority of actions which are actually heard, terminate in a judgment, and the great majority of such judgments are for the payment of sums of money. The principal method of having such a judgment debt enforced is to have the property of the defendant seized and sold. This is done by making an order, called an order of *fieri-facias*, directed to the Sheriff (or county registrar), commanding him to levy the amount of the judgment with interest on the defendant's goods. It is also possible to 'attach' a person who fails to comply with a judgment, i.e. to commit him to prison for contempt in failing to comply with it. A judgment for the recovery of land, or other specific property, is also directed to the Sheriff (or county registrar), and in the case of land which is owned by the defendant, this can be made available for the satisfaction of the judgment by registering a 'judgment mortgage' against it.

Since 1926, 'attachment' proceedings in the High Court have been rare, for under the Enforcement of Court Orders Act 1926, judgment debtors may be examined as to their means in the District Court. Once this examination has been completed, the judgment creditor may apply to the District Court for an order directing that the amount due be paid by instalments.

Appeals to the Supreme Court

Article 34 of the Constitution states that the Supreme Court is the appellate tribunal for all proceedings commenced in the High

Court and all constitutional cases, wherever started. It has also certain jurisdiction of an appellate nature from inferior courts, which has been conferred by statute. [1] In hearing appeals, it takes the evidence from the shorthand note made at the trial; witnesses are not examined before it. In appeals from verdicts of a judge sitting alone, an appellant may ask for the original verdict to be reversed, and the Supreme Court may make any order that the trial judge might have made. Not only are the trial judge's decisions on law open to review but also his findings of fact. But, as a matter of practice, the Supreme Court will be slower to interfere with a finding of fact based on the observation of a witness in the actual trial than one based on documents or on inference from established facts. In appeals from judgments of the High Court founded on the verdict of a jury, the appellant can ask only for a new trial. However, in lieu of ordering a retrial, the Supreme Court may set aside the verdict, findings and judgment, and substitute some other judgment. If the Supreme Court orders a retrial before another jury, the unsuccessful party will have to pay the costs of two trials and one appeal. An appeal from a jury verdict may be based on the ground that the judge misdirected the jury in law or as to evidence, that the damages were excessive or inadequate, or that the verdict was against the weight of evidence. But where a finding of fact has been left to a jury at a trial, the Supreme Court will not disturb it if it is one reasonably open on the evidence. This makes appeal much more difficult in jury than in non-jury cases.

In addition to its appellate jurisdiction, the Supreme Court also has some original jurisdiction under the Constitution. Article 12 provides that only the Supreme Court, consisting of not less than five judges, can establish the permanent incapacity of the President of Ireland. Article 26 gives the Supreme Court jurisdiction to decide whether any provision of a Bill referred to it by the President of Ireland is repugnant to the Constitution. The Committee on Court Practice and Procedure in its Eleventh Interim Report suggested that there should also be expressly conferred on the Supreme Court jurisdiction to try in the first instance, on consent of the parties, net constitutional issues initiated in the High Court concerning the validity of Acts of the Oireachtas, or any other

[1] See Workmen's Compensation Act 1934, Section 36. Also *The State (Browne)* v. *Feran* (1967] I.R. 147 and *Vella* v. *Morelli* [1968] I.R. 11.

net issue of law of importance in cases in which no decision on any disputed question of fact is required.

Appeals to European Courts

By virtue of Article 177 of the Treaty of Rome, the Court of Justice of the European Communities has jurisdiction to give preliminary rulings on questions of the interpretation of the Treaty and certain other related matters. If such a question is raised before a domestic court, that court may request the Court of Justice to give a ruling. If the court before which the question is raised is one from which there is no appeal at internal law in the particular case, that court is bound to bring the matter before the Court of Justice.

Under the European Convention on Human Rights, to which Ireland is a party, an injured person may petition the European Commission of Human Rights on the ground that a state party has violated the rights set forth in the Convention. Such a petition is not admissible unless the injured party has exhausted all possible remedies before the domestic courts. If it is declared admissible, the matter is investigated *in camera* by the Commission, which is charged to attempt to secure a friendly settlement. If this is not achieved, the Commission draws up a report stating whether the facts found disclose a breach by the state concerned of its obligations under the Convention. The Commission or any party may refer the case to the European Court of Human Rights which is empowered to afford satisfaction to an injured person. Otherwise the report is considered by the Committee of Ministers of the Council of Europe who decide if there has been a violation of the Convention and, if there has been, it may prescribe the measures to be taken by the state which is guilty of such violation. One of the first cases brought under this Convention was an unsuccessful petition by one Gerard Lawless who had been interned during the IRA campaign of the late nineteen fifties. Since that time, there have been remarkably few petitions from Ireland under the Convention. However, the Convention has played an important role in Northern Ireland Affairs. In 1971 the Irish government, availing of its rights as a party to the Convention, referred to the European Commission of Human Rights the ill-treatment of detained persons and other alleged violations of the Convention by the British government in Northern Ireland.

Inferior Courts

The jurisdiction of the High Court is unlimited and, as successor to the whole series of superior courts existing in Ireland before 1877, it can try all matters and causes of a civil nature, without limitation of territory or amount involved. The Circuit and District Courts, on the other hand, are creatures of statute and were set up under the Courts of Justice Act 1924 to absorb the previously existing jurisdiction of the old County Courts and the Courts of Petty Sessions, and also to take over so much of the High Court jurisdiction as related to the everyday legal business of the country which ought to be disposed of locally. Article 34 of the 1937 Constitution, having provided that the Courts of First Instance should include a High Court invested with full original jurisdiction to determine all matters and questions, whether of law or fact, went on to say that there should also be courts of local and limited jurisdiction. The Circuit and District Courts function under this Article.

(i) The Circuit Court

The jurisdiction of the Circuit Court is confined to those matters assigned to it by statute and particularly the Courts (Supplemental Provisions) Act 1961 as amended by the Courts Act 1971. This jurisdiction extends to

(a) actions founded on contract and tort where the claim does not exceed £2,000;

(b) actions in which the title to land comes into question, where the Poor Law Valuation of the land does not exceed £100;

(c) actions in relation to the grant of probate of a will or letters of administration of a deceased person where the estate of the deceased person consists of personalty whose value is not more than £5,000 or land whose Poor Law Valuation is not more than £100;

(d) equity suits, e.g. proceedings for the dissolution of partnerships, the redemption of mortgages, the execution of trusts, the partition or sale of land, the rectification of deeds, specific performance, injunctions, where the subject-matter does not exceed £5,000 in personalty or include land of a Poor Law Valuation greater than £100;

(e) proceedings at the suit of the state or any minister or government department where the amount due or recoverable does not exceed £2,000.

Proceedings involving a subject-matter in excess of the limits of jurisdiction laid down by statute for the Circuit Court may, nonetheless, be litigated in that court, where the parties to the proceedings consent in writing. This meets the occasional desire of parties to dispose of comparatively large claims rapidly, locally and with a minimum of formality, particularly for the recovery of debts of a simple nature. The Committee on Court Practice and Procedure, in its Fifth Interim Report, suggested that this consent jurisdiction should be encouraged, but one member drew attention to the constitutional difficulties of conferring such unlimited jurisdiction on an inferior court.

Provision is made under the appropriate statutes for the transfer from the High Court to the Circuit Court (or, where necessary, to the District Court) of actions that might have been commenced before the latter tribunals. The bringing of an action in the High Court by a plaintiff who might have commenced his proceedings in the Circuit Court may result in his being awarded costs on the Circuit Court scale only.

The Circuit Court has exclusive jurisdiction over certain categories of cases, irrespective of the value of the subject-matter or the amount of the claim. It is the court for the hearing of applications for new on-licences and new club licences, for claims under the Criminal Injuries code, for certain categories of ejectment actions, and for applications for new leases under the Landlord and Tenant Acts 1931 and 1958. Contrariwise, there are classes of cases, such as petitions to wind up companies and matrimonial causes (including actions for criminal conversation), that are completely excluded from the original jurisdiction of the Circuit Court.

Like the High Court, the practice and procedure of the Circuit Court is regulated by rules made by a statutory Circuit Court Rules Committee. Since the Circuit Court replaced the old County Courts, it is natural that one should find that the 'civil bill' procedure is the basis of the practice of this court. The civil bill is drawn in such a way as to set forth a simple statement of the plaintiff's claim, and, unlike the summons in the High Court, is served on the defendant by a court official. The defendant thereupon enters an appearance and files a defence, stating clearly the grounds on which he disputes the plaintiff's claim. There is also provision in the Circuit Court for a 'default judgment' procedure, analogous to the High Court, on the basis that the defendant has not lodged either an appearance or a defence. The High Court practice of allowing a plaintiff to obtain summary judgment on his affidavit that he believes that there is no bona fide defence to his claim is also followed in the Circuit Court.

While the system of pleading in the Circuit Court is simpler and more expeditious than that existing in the High Court, it is, nonetheless, more complex than that which prevailed in the old County Courts. This is, perhaps, attributable to the fact that it has an enhanced jurisdiction, and also to the fact that, since 1924, counsel have to an increasing extent exercised their right of audience there.

Generally speaking, an appeal lies to the High Court from decisions in cases originating in the Circuit Court. For this purpose the state is divided into a number of 'High Court Circuits', and twice a year judges of the High Court sit in each county and county borough to hear these appeals. If the appeal is from the Dublin Circuit Court, or from a Circuit Court action elsewhere in which there is no oral evidence, it is heard by the High Court sitting in Dublin. Except in cases where no oral evidence was heard in the Circuit Court, there is a complete rehearing of the evidence. Section 39 of the Courts of Justice Act 1936 provides that the decision of the High Court on an appeal from the Circuit Court is "final and conclusive and not appealable." However, on the hearing of such an appeal, the High Court may, on the application of any party, state a case for the opinion of the Supreme Court on any question of law and may adjourn the hearing of the appeal pending the determination of such case stated.

There are exceptions to this normal channel of appeal from verdicts of the Circuit Court. Parties to a case before the court may agree that its decision should be final. In income tax cases there is no appeal from findings of fact of a Circuit Court judge —on questions of law there is an appeal to the High Court and thence to the Supreme Court. Under the Workmen's Compensation Act 1934, an appeal lies directly from the Circuit Court to the Supreme Court. By virtue of Section 16 of the Courts of Justice Act 1947, a judge of the Circuit Court is empowered to refer any question of law arising in a matter pending before him to the Supreme Court by way of case stated. [2]

The special position of the Circuit Court judge assigned to the Cork Circuit should be noted. He constitutes the Cork Local Admiralty Court and the Cork Local Bankruptcy Court. The latter has the same jurisdiction as the High Court in respect of persons residing or carrying on business on the Circuit.

(ii) The District Court

Apart from certain minor civil jurisdiction (which was exercised by Courts of Petty Session in Ireland) with respect to the recovery of small debts, the determination of disputes concerning rent, and some jurisdiction in ejectments, the principal civil jurisdiction exercised by the District Court was conferred upon it *de novo* in 1924, when the Court was first set up. This jurisdiction has been developed by subsequent legislation, bearing in mind the desirability of maintaining the essential character of the Court as a tribunal of simple procedure for small cases. The Courts Act 1971 represented a real as well as a monetary addition to the limits of the District Court's jurisdiction.

The District Court's general civil jurisdiction extends

(i) in contract and tort to all actions where the claim does not exceed £250, except for defamation, seduction, false imprisonment, malicious prosecution and criminal conversation, all of which are excluded from its purview;

(ii) in ejectment for non-payment of rent, or overholding where the rent does not exceed £315 per annum;

(iii) in proceedings at the suit of the state, or any official thereof, where the amount involved does not exceed £250.

In addition, specific jurisdiction has been conferred on the District Court by particular statutes, e.g. The Illegitimate Children (Affiliation Orders) Act 1930, The Hire Purchase Acts 1946 and 1960, The Rent Restrictions Act 1960, The Hotel Proprietors Act 1963. It has unlimited jurisdiction in all licensing matters except for new on-licences and new club licences, which are reserved to the Circuit Court. Similarly, no limit is provided in the case of summary proceedings for the payment of rates. In contrast to the Circuit Court, which has no competence in matrimonial matters,

[2] *The People (Attorney General)* v. *McGlynn* [1967] I.R. 147.

the District Court has a long-standing and much exercised jurisdiction to award maintenance to deserted wives. Under the Courts
Act 1971, this important jurisdiction is confined to awards of £15
per week to the deserted wife and £5 for each dependent child,
but a wife can also apply to the High Court which has unlimited
jurisdiction. No action has yet been taken on the recommendation
of the Committee on Court Practice and Procedure, contained in
its Nineteenth Interim Report published in February 1974, that
the jurisdiction of the District Court should no longer be restricted
to the sums mentioned in the 1971 Act. It was, said the Committee,
the most suitable forum for hearing desertion cases. In other
respects, the District Court has more restricted scope than the
Circuit Court. It has no jurisdiction whatsoever to determine the
title to land or in equity matters. Parties before it are not permitted
to extend its jurisdiction by mutual consent.

Civil proceedings in the District Court are begun by the issue
and service of a 'Civil Process'. No defence is filed, but the
defendant must enter a 'notice of intention to defend'. There is a
'default' procedure in the case of actions for debt or for a liquidated
money demand.

Generally speaking, appeals from the District Court lie to the
Circuit Court. The latter rehears the whole case and its decision
is then final on fact. There may be an appeal to the High Court
by 'case stated' on a point of law, and, by leave of that Court, a
further appeal on the point to the Supreme Court. By virtue of
Section 52 of the Courts (Supplemental Provisions) Act 1961, this
process may be short-circuited. Provision is made for the District
Justice, on his own initiative or at the request of one of the parties,
to refer questions of law arising in proceedings before him to
the High Court for determination. An appeal then lies to the
Supreme Court, but only by leave of the High Court. This requirement of leave to appeal to the Supreme Court in District Court
cases was criticised by the Committee on Court Practice and
Procedure, in its Eleventh Interim Report published in March
1970. The Committee also suggested that the District Court should
have power to refer any constitutional cases arising before it direct
to the Supreme Court for determination. No action has yet been
taken on either of these recommendations.

Courts Exercising Civil Jurisdiction

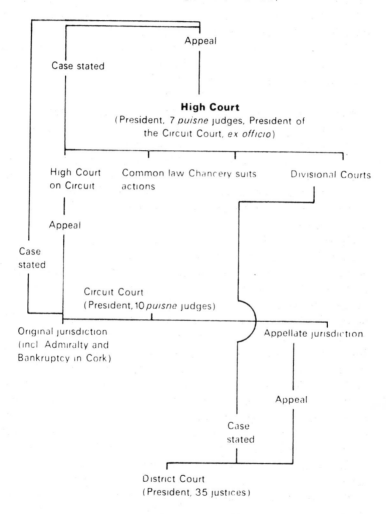

Supreme Court *
(Chief Justice, 4 *puisne* judges, President
of the High Court, *ex officio*)

Appeal

Case stated

High Court
(President, 7 *puisne* judges, President of
the Circuit Court, *ex officio*)

High Court   Common law Chancery suits   Divisional Courts
on Circuit   actions

Appeal

Case
stated

Circuit Court
(President, 10 *puisne* judges)

Original jurisdiction   Appellate jurisdiction
(incl. Admiralty and
Bankruptcy in Cork)

Appeal

Case
stated

District Court
(President, 35 justices)

CHAPTER VIII

THE PERSONNEL OF THE COURTS

The Judiciary

At the present time, justice is administered in the Courts of the Republic of Ireland by the judges of the Supreme Court and the High Court, the judges of the Circuit Court, and the justices of the District Court. In the Supreme Court, there is the Chief Justice, with four puisne or ordinary judges. By statute there are ten judges of the Circuit Court and thirty-five justices of the District Court including in each case, their respective presidents. These are supplemented by temporary judges and justices appointed by virtue of Section 51 of the Courts of Justice Act 1936.

The principle of security of tenure for judges is long established in these islands and is an important bulwark of judicial independence. In England and Wales, since the Act of Settlement 1701, every judge holds office for life, "subject to a power of removal by Her Majesty the Queen on an address presented to Her Majesty by both Houses of Parliament." There may be a petition to either House, though there is some authority for saying that it must originate in the Commons. The charge against the judge would have to be formulated and he would have to be given an opportunity of defending it. No English judge has been removed since 1701, so the matter has never arisen for determination.

Although a number of attempts were made by the Irish Parliament to secure similar fixity of tenure for the judges in Ireland, it was not until 1782 that the statute 21 & 22 Geo. III c. 11 was passed, conferring the same privilege on the judges here. The Judicature (Ir.) Act 1877 repeated the formula of the Act of Settlement, and this pertained until 1924.

Article 68 of the Constitution of the Irish Free State 1922 provided that all judges should be appointed by the Governor General on the advice of the Executive Council, and should not be removed "except for stated misbehaviour or incapacity," and then only by resolutions passed by both Houses of the Oireachtas. The Article also made provision for the fixing of a retiring age for judges, and referred not only to the Supreme Court and High Court judges, but also to "all other courts established" under the Constitution.

When the new courts were set up by the Courts of Justice Act 1924, it was provided that Circuit Court judges were to hold office by the same tenure as the judges of the High and Supreme Courts, but District Justices were made removable for incapacity, physical or mental infirmity, or misbehaviour in office, by a certificate to that effect signed by the Attorney General and the Chief Justice. This remained the position with regard to District Justices until 1946, when they were given the same tenure as the judges of the other courts.

The Constitution of Ireland 1937 provides (articles 13(9) and 35(1)) that the judges of all courts shall be appointed by the President on the advice of the government, and it repeats the procedure for removal contained in the 1922 Constitution, namely by the President on a resolution of both Houses of the Oireachtas. All persons appointed to judicial office must make a solemn declaration before assuming office, and under the provisions of the Courts (Establishment and Constitution) Act 1961, a judicial office held by any person may be resigned by a communication in writing addressed to the President.

With regard to the District Court, the Courts of Justice (District Court) Act 1946, s. 21, provides a machinery whereby the Minister for Justice may request the Chief Justice to appoint a judge to investigate the condition of health, or the conduct of a district justice, and report to the minister, while under the Courts (Supplemental Provisions) Act 1961, the Chief Justice may interview privately a justice of the District Court in relation to conduct which he considers to be such as to bring the administration of justice into disrepute and may "inform him of such opinion."

Before the constitutional changes of 1920-1922, and after the Act of Union, the situation in Ireland was that the judges of the superior courts were appointed by the Prime Minister. In England, appointments to the puisne judgeships in the High Court were (and are still) made by the Lord Chancellor, the function of the Prime Minister being confined to the Law Lords, the Lords Justices, the Lord Chief Justice, the Master of the Rolls, and the President of the Probate, Divorce and Admiralty Division. So far as the Irish appointments were concerned, however, the Irish Lord Chancellor does not seem to have had any formal voice in them, though he frequently claimed this privilege. The Irish Lord Chancellor himself, of course, was appointed by the government in office and had to vacate his place on a change of ministry. Normally, he was a member of the English bar, and until the Whig government appointed Maziere Brady to the post in 1846, no Irishman had occupied it for many years.

Politics played a considerable part in the preferment of men to the Bench in Ireland. Of those who were appointed to judgeships between 1801 and 1921, over half had sat in the House of Commons and nearly three-quarters had been law officers—either Attorney General or Solicitor General—and so had been in the forefront of political activity, since the function of the law officers was to advise the government in legal matters. In England, it is only right to say, the situation was not dissimilar until recent times. Out of 139 appointments made to the Bench between 1832 and 1906, 80 of those appointed were members of Parliament at the time of their appointment, and of these, 63 were appointed while their party was in office, leaving 17 appointments made from those in political opposition.

The urge to ascend the Bench in Ireland in the nineteenth century was stimulated by the fact that it was a very valuable prize. The Lord Chancellor enjoyed an income of £10,000 until 1832, when it was fixed at £8,000. After 1877, the Lord Chief Justice of Ireland received £5,000, the other heads of Divisions £4,500, while the puisne judges could look forward to a salary of about £3,500. There was provision made for the judges to retire on pension, but there was no compulsory retiring age. Lord Norbury retired from the Bench at the age of eighty-eight, and Chief Justice Lefroy, who had been promoted from the Exchequer at the age of seventy-six, resigned in his ninety-first year. A motion in the Commons to remove him for incapacity resulted in his being defended by his son, then a member of Parliament in his sixties. One judge of the Irish High Court of Admiralty, Jonah Barrington, was removed from office in rather discreditable circumstances, this being the only occasion on which the procedure has ever been carried out.

In the courts of local jurisdiction, there was not the same fixity of tenure. At first, the assistant barrister was paid a salary not exceeding £300 a year, and was appointed and removed by the Lord Lieutenant. Later, he was made removable only by the Crown on an address of both Houses, with the proviso that in case of incapacity, the Lord Lieutenant could remove him by order in council. The salaries of resident magistrates started at about £400, but were later raised to the region of £700 a year. They, too, were appointed and removed by the Lord Lieutenant.

When the new courts were established in 1924, all the judges of the old Supreme Court of Judicature in Southern Ireland retired. The Executive Council was faced with the choice of asking some of the outgoing judges to take office in the new courts or of appointing an entirely fresh judiciary. In the event, they adopted a compromise, and two of the former judges—Charles O'Connor, the Master of the Rolls, and Mr Justice Wylie—were appointed judges of the Supreme Court and the High Court respectively. In addition two of the new judges—Mr Justice O'Shaughnessy and Mr Justice Johnston—had been judges in inferior courts under the old régime while another—Mr Justice Hanna—had been Third Sergeant. The remainder were drawn from the members of the practising Bar, and the new Chief Justice, Hugh Kennedy, had been Law Officer for the Irish Free State.

The salaries paid to the new judiciary were modest by previous standards. The Chief Justice received £4,000 per annum, the ordinary judges of the Supreme Court and the President of the High Court received £3,000, while the ordinary judges of the High Court were paid £2,500. In the Circuit Court, the judicial salary was £1,700, while District Justices received salaries ranging from £1,000 to £1,200. These salaries have not always been readjusted promptly or adequately to reflect the changing value of money. At times it has seemed that the government were failing to honour the spirit of the constitutional provision that the remuneration of a judge shall not be reduced during his continuance in office. There has also been a tendency to narrow the differential between the different categories of judges. Since 1 March 1975 the Chief Justice receives £14,210; the President of the High Court £12,315; each ordinary judge of the Supreme Court £11,999; each ordinary member of the High Court £10,419; the President of the Circuit

Court £10,419; each ordinary judge of the Circuit Court £8,652; the President of the District Court £8,773; each District Justice £6,757. The rates, especially for the higher judges, are low compared with those in Britain. However, they have not proved inadequate to attract leaders of the Bar to senior judicial appointments.

With regard to tenure of office, the new system of courts established in 1924 introduced a system of retiring ages. This is seventy-two years in the case of the Supreme Court and the High Court, seventy years in the case of the Circuit Court (but seventy-two for its President), and sixty-five years in the case of the District Court.

When one comes to investigate the system of appointments to judicial office in the Republic of Ireland, the legislation is not very informative. Qualifications of a formal type are laid down, but nothing more is prescribed. Thus, a practising barrister of not less than twelve years' standing is qualified for appointment to the Supreme Court or the High Court, and a similar qualification of ten years' standing is necessary for the Circuit Court. In the District Court, barristers or solicitors who have actually practised their professions for not less than ten years are eligible for appointment.

The actual selection of the candidate is left to the government. As a matter of tradition, it is said that the Attorney General has certain claims on the first refusal of every judgeship falling vacant during his period of office. This is a survival of the days when appointments to this post were made from senior members of the Inner Bar who were active lawyer-politicians. In fact, recent Attorney Generals have seemed less anxious to go on the Bench than their predecessors.

There is much to be said for the view that the present system of leaving the selection of the judiciary in the hands of the government is open to many objections. The qualities which make a man a good judge may not be those which commend themselves or are even apparent to the politician, and, as between two candidates of equal merit, it is only human nature that party loyalty should become the deciding factor. There is, in the words of an eminent constitutional lawyer, Professor Dicey, "an irresistible temptation to appoint magistrates who agree (honestly, it may be) with the views of the Executive." Dicey was speaking of the working of the Constitution of the United States, but the same danger can exist in Ireland. This was foreseen by Professor Swift MacNeill, in his work on the

Constitution of the Irish Free State, when he observed on the "tendency to make the selection under such circumstances on the ground more of political services than professional merit."

Appointment to the Bench by the government inevitably exposes the judiciary to the danger of having persons appointed to it whose qualifications are defective. Secondly, it exposes individual members of the government to unwonted pressures from all sorts of sources. Finally, it can have the most detrimental effect on the Bar as a professional body. It has been suggested that a possible solution to the difficulty is that either the Benchers of the Society of King's Inns might be constituted a selection body, or that the general body of the judges of the particular court in which the vacancy is to be filled might be appointed to act on a basis of co-option. Alternatively, the non-judicial Benchers might draw up a panel of names from which the judges could make a selection. The constitutional requirement that all judicial appointments shall be made on the advice of the government would in no way preclude the setting up of a statutory selection body for the purpose of advising the government, and the establishment of a convention whereby the guidance so offered should be followed. There are precedents for this development, in the case of appointments to offices formerly in the gift of the Crown, and now filled by the government: and in at least one instance, the advice of the society of which the officer is the titular head has invariably been accepted.

The Organisation of Court Sittings

The arrangement and distribution of the business of the courts is governed by a comprehensive set of statutory provisions, and the whole question of court 'sittings' is one of considerable antiquity. The history of the 'legal year', indeed, may be traced back to the Anglo-Saxon period in England, and this system of sittings of the courts interspersed with vacations was taken over by the Normans, who imported it into Ireland.

Under this system, the legal year was divided into four 'terms.' Hilary Term began early in January and ended before Easter. Easter Term began eight days after Easter Day and ended on the eve of Ascension Day. Trinity Term began eight days after Whit Sunday and ended about 12 July. Michaelmas Term began on the Tuesday after Michaelmas Day and ended with the commencement of

Advent. As time went on, these periods were regulated by statute, and by the middle of the nineteenth century in Ireland, Hilary Term ran from 11 to 31 January; Easter Term from 15 April to 8 May; Trinity Term from 22 May to 12 June; and Michaelmas Term from 2 to 25 November.

It will be observed that these sittings were very short, and so it was impossible to transact all the legal business during term time. In addition, all actions tried before the common law courts, whether coming before them at Dublin or on Assize, had to go before the whole Court of Queen's Bench, Common Pleas, or Exchequer, as the case might be, sitting *in banc*. Once the jury had returned a judgment on an issue of fact, the judge might order a verdict to be entered for the plaintiff or the defender, but he never ordered judgment to be entered. The judge sitting at *nisi prius* was merely superintending the trial, as this was a more convenient way of conducting the trial than holding it before the full court. He might, for instance, reserve a legal point to be argued before the full court, and a rule of practice developed that the decision of one judge sitting at *nisi prius* did not bind another, a rule which still technically applies, even though now the trial judge does enter judgment.

The effect of all this was to develop a system of 'after sittings' of the courts, out of term, in which cases heard at *nisi prius* could come before the courts sitting *in banc* for judgment, and this was given statutory recognition in Ireland in 1856. Before that, sittings *in banc* could only be held in term, while sittings at *nisi prius* and at the Assizes were held out of term.

The Judicature (Ir.) Act 1877 abolished 'terms' as such, so far as they related to the administration of justice. There is now a system of 'sittings', four in every calendar year, called Hilary, Easter, Trinity and Michaelmas Sittings, with four 'vacations' (Easter, Whitsun, Long (or Summer), and Christmas) between them. The sittings are now: Hilary, 11 January (or, if it falls on Saturday or Sunday, the following Monday) to Saturday before Holy Week; Easter, Monday after Easter Week to Thursday before Whit Sunday; Trinity, Wednesday after Whitsun week to 31 July; and Michaelmas, first Monday in October to 21 December.

In addition to these sittings of the judges of the High Court in Dublin for the dispatch of civil business, the Court of Criminal Appeal also sits there: and the Supreme Court disposes of the cases coming before it as the occasion demands. Since 1936, it will be recalled, appeals from the Circuit Court are heard by the judges of the High Court, travelling a number of circuits comprising groups of counties and county boroughs. These circuits now go out in March and November in order to hear Circuit Court appeals.

As far as the Circuit Court is concerned, the state is divided into a series of eight circuits, one of which is called the Dublin Circuit and includes the county and county borough of Dublin, and another —the Cork Circuit which includes the county and county borough of Cork. Four judges (including two temporary judges) are assigned to the Dublin Circuit and one judge to each of the others.

The District Court sittings are administered by a grouping of the state into a number of districts. There is a Dublin Metropolitan District, and the Minister for Justice has comprehensive powers to create new districts, amalgamate districts, and make such changes as may be necessary.

The Officers of the Courts

By the beginning of the nineteenth century the superior courts in Dublin had acquired a very extensive administrative service. Each of the three common law courts, the Court of Chancery, and the other courts had a staff of officials, charged with the duty of preparing writs and summonses, taking affidavits, filing documents, enrolling judgments, taxing costs, and collecting fines.

The Court of Chancery, apart from the Lord Chancellor and the Master of the Rolls, had four Masters in Chancery whose work was quasi-judicial and whose remuneration was almost that of a common law judge. Each Master had a staff consisting of an Examiner, a Clerk, and an Examiner's Clerk. There were also the 'Six Clerks' who acted as agents for the solicitors practising in the Court of Chancery and who had a staff to assist them; the Examiners, the Accountant-General, the Cursitor, the Registrars, the Usher and the Serjeant-at-arms. In all, the Court of Chancery employed a staff of eighty-five persons.

The Queen's Bench had on the civil side sixteen officials employing fourteen clerks, and on the Crown side three officials, making a total staff of thirty-three. The Court of Common Pleas had a staff of thirty-six, while the Court of Exchequer had a staff of sixty-nine.

In the three common law courts, the best remunerated officials were sinecurists, their duties being performed by deputies appointed by themselves. Some of the offices were in the gift of the Crown, while the judges and the senior officials all had rights of patronage. In all, there were employed at the Four Courts about a hundred and seventeen officials, who themselves appointed and paid over a hundred clerks. The tenure of office of these court officials varied: it might be at pleasure, for good behaviour, or for life. But, as has been pointed out elsewhere, "no office holder, unless guilty of grave malversation, should be compelled to relinquish his post." The income of these officials greatly varied, since they were remunerated from fees; but a net income of about £4,000 per annum was not uncommon.

As a result of repeated complaints about the management of the affairs of the Irish courts, a commission was set up in 1815 to investigate their working, and this body completed its deliberations in 1831, having presented twenty-two reports. As a result, a number of reforms were carried out in the administrative machinery, and the Judicature Act completed this task in 1877 by making provision for a unified staff of the new Supreme Court of Judicature in Ireland. Provision was made for the recruitment of staff of certain grades by open competition, but as the judges preserved their rights of patronage, it was not until 1903 that the first official was, in fact, appointed in this way.

The arrangements for the staffing and administration of the courts in existence in Ireland between 1877 and 1921 were a considerable improvement on what had gone before, but the details and organisation were still extremely complex. Thus, in the Chancery Division, there were still the following departments, each with its appropriate staff: the Office of the Clerk of the Crown and Hanaper; the Office of the Chief Clerk; the Receiver Office; the Chancery Registrar's Office; the Land Registry; the Judgment, Record and Writ Office; the Consolidated Taxing Office; and the Consolidated Accounting Office. In the King's Bench Division there were: the Master of the King's Bench Division (with twenty-six officials); the Clerk of the Crown; and the Chief Registrar of the King's Bench Division (Probate). In all, the courts in Dublin still required the services of a hundred and ten officials.

When the new courts were established in 1924, the opportunity was taken to recast the whole system of officials. The Court Officers

Act 1926 dealt with the matter by abolishing all existing offices and officers in the various divisions of the old High Court, and creating new offices with new officials, mainly transferred, but with new descriptive titles. In the High Court, one Central Office was set up, controlled and administered by a new official called the Master of the High Court who, as has been pointed out in an earlier chapter, has certain quasi-judicial functions. The Master of the High Court has complete superintendence and control of the administrative side of the High Court, except for probate and bankruptcy business, which are still under separate direction, and except also for the Accountant and the Examiner (formerly the Chief Clerk in the Chancery Division). There is a partial retention of control of the staffs of the court by the judiciary, in so far as it is provided that no officer can be removed from office without the concurrence of the Chief Justice and the President of the High Court. Moreover, since 1936, the functions of the Chief Justice with regard to persons of unsound mind and minors have been vested in the President of the High Court, and the administrative side of this jurisdiction is performed by the Office of Wards of Court.

So far as the courts of limited jurisdiction were concerned, the position was that at the beginning of the nineteenth century, each county in Ireland had an officer called the Clerk of the Crown, who was responsible for the functioning of the Courts of Assize and who kept their records. The Clerk of the Peace carried out parallel functions for the Courts of Quarter Sessions, and he was also principal officer in the Assistant-Barrister's Court. The Clerk of the Crown was appointed by letters patent, while the Clerk of the Peace was appointed by the Lord Lieutenant and *Custos Rotulorum* of the county. The Crown claimed the right to appoint the latter officer, however, and in 1819 this claim was challenged in a case about an appointment for King's County, which ultimately went to the House of Lords and was decided in favour of the appointment by the *Custos Rotulorum*. [1]

In 1877 the County Officers and Courts (Ir.) Act provided for the amalgamation of these two offices, by empowering the Lord Lieutenant to appoint a Clerk of the Crown and Peace for each county as vacancies occurred. He was to be paid a salary fixed by

[1] *Harding v. Pollock* (1829) 3 Bligh N.S. 161.

the Act and was to be removable by the Lord Chancellor. The statute also made provision for the appointment of Registrars to be attached to each County Court for civil business.

In 1926, the legislation regulating court officers provided for the establishment of a Circuit Court Office for every county and county borough. The office of Clerk of the Crown and Peace and that of Registrar of a Civil Bill Court were abolished and a new official was created, called the 'County Registrar,' who now discharges all the administrative functions of a registrar in the Circuit Court on both its civil and criminal side. Arrangements were also made to transfer the functions of the Under-Sheriffs to the County Registrars as vacancies arose: these functions are now exercised by County Registrars everywhere except in Cork County and County Borough and Dublin County and County Borough where they are performed by sheriffs appointed under the Court Officers Act 1945.

So far as the Courts of Petty Sessions were concerned, in 1827 it was enacted that the Justices of the Peace meeting in sessions might appoint a clerk who was to be paid out of fees collected by the Court. In 1858, these Petty Sessions clerks were made salaried officials, and from then onwards there were about 600 Petty Sessions districts in Ireland, each with its own clerk. After the District Court was set up, a new office of 'District Court Clerk' was created to discharge these functions for any District Court area constituted in replacement of a Court of Petty Sessions.

It remains to say something of the old law officers of the Crown, who vanished with the political changes in 1921-1922. These were the Prime Serjeant, the Attorney General, the Solicitor General, and the King's Advocate (who acted for the Crown in Admiralty cases). The Prime Serjeant's office was allowed to lapse after the death of the last holder in 1805, but there did survive three 'King's Serjeants', appointed under letters patent, who conducted Crown business, and ranked after the Attorney General and the Solicitor General. These serjeants had no exact equivalent in England, where the serjeants-at-law constituted a separate rank of counsel and were abolished after the Judicature Acts. They survived in Ireland down to 1921.

The Irish law officers exercised a considerable influence in the government of the country. The Attorney General was almost invariably a Privy Councillor, and he seems to have had a very substantial influence on the making of policy. In addition, as a member of Parliament, he was available at Westminster to answer for Irish affairs, in the absence of the Chief Secretary.

When the Irish Free State was set up in 1922, no constitutional provision was made for an Attorney General, and between 1922 and 1924 the legal adviser to the government was described as the Law Officer. In 1924, under the Ministers and Secretaries Act, a new office of Attorney General was created. He was never a member of the cabinet, however, and the office was regarded as non-political, though in the gift of the government in power for the time being.

Special provision is now made for the Attorney General in Article 30 of the Constitution. He is adviser on matters of law and legal opinion to the government but is not a member of it nor is he invariably a member of the Oireachtas. He is nominated by the Taoiseach and retires with him. Before the coming into force of the Prosecution of Offences Act 1974, all prosecutions on indictment were conducted at his suit in the name of the People. He conducts civil litigation on behalf of the government. However, it has never been the custom for the Attorney General to appear personally in either category of case. He also acts as leader of the Bar and some holders of the office have managed to carry on lucrative private practices.

CHAPTER IX

THE LEGAL PROFESSION

As might have been expected from the parallel course of development in the courts and the system of legal rules, the profession of the law in Ireland has developed along similar lines to those followed in England. Here, as in England, the profession is divided into two branches, solicitors and barristers, and it will be proper, at the outset, to describe each of these groups of organised lawyers.

The Solicitor

The distinct profession of a solicitor developed in England at a comparatively recent date. Originally, the barristers constituted the whole body of the legal profession, and those clerks who eventually evolved into the modern solicitor were then comparatively unimportant. The Court of King's Bench and the Court of Common Pleas had associated with them a number of officials known as 'attorneys', appointed and controlled by the judges, whose task it was to represent clients in the preliminary stages of litigation. The work of the attorney was purely mechanical and the more highly skilled business of conducting cases in court was left to the barrister. In the Court of Chancery, a similar class of person developed. They were called 'solicitors', and they corresponded to the attorneys in the common law courts. In addition, the Admiralty and Ecclesiastical Courts had officials of this type called 'proctors'.

At first, the attorneys in London shared with the members of the Bar the Inns of Court where the latter were constituted into a professional body. But in the eighteenth century the attorneys formed their own professional organisation, to which attorneys, solicitors and proctors could belong. The men practising in London were generally solicitors as well as attorneys; the disappearance of the Ecclesiastical Courts led to the extinction of the separate class of proctors, and there grew up a combined profession calling itself that of 'solicitor'.

In Ireland, the profession developed along similar lines. When the Honourable Society of King's Inns, the barristers' society, was reconstituted in 1607, membership was made up of the judiciary, the bar and the attorneys. Later, in 1792, when the society obtained a royal charter of incorporation (later cancelled), it was given absolute power both over the Bar and over the attorneys and solicitors, and it was confirmed by a statute which provided, *inter alia*, that one of the duties of the new body was to make rules and orders for the admission of persons to learn the business of attorneys. This arrangement lasted down to 1866, though, in fact, nothing was done by the society to educate attorneys for their profession.

In 1861, a number of attorneys practising in the city of Dublin met together and formed The Society of Attorneys and Solicitors of Ireland, with the object of improving the educational and professional standards of their body. This was the direct successor of two earlier organisations, the Law Club of Ireland, formed in 1791, and the Law Society of Ireland, founded in 1830.

This new society remained subsidiary to but independent of the Benchers of King's Inns, and had no power to alter or amend the existing regulations concerning education. It continued to flourish as a body controlling professional conduct, however, and in 1852, it obtained a charter of incorporation under the name of The Incorporated Society of the Attorneys and Solicitors of Ireland. Following long and fruitless negotiations with the Benchers, the society obtained legislation in 1866, enabling it to exercise complete control over the legal education of attorneys' apprentices. It was no longer necessary for an attorney to become a member of King's Inns, and, in 1898, complete disciplinary power over the profession was conferred on the Incorporated Law Society of Ireland, as it is now termed.

From the earliest times, admission to the profession of a solicitor has been based on a combination of practical training as an apprentice and examinations. At present this is for a period of five years, though it may be abridged to three years in the case of a university graduate in arts or law who has proceeded to his degree before being bound as an apprentice, or to four years in the case of a matriculated university student who graduates in a university in the Republic of Ireland after entering upon articles of apprenticeship, or who attends certain courses in law at certain prescribed universities. Courses of lectures, which are compulsory, are provided by the Incorporated Law Society, and there are three law examinations before admission to practice, and two examinations in the Irish language.

Since solicitors are traditionally officers of the courts, they are amenable to the direct discipline of the judiciary, and there is an inherent power in the High Court to compel a solicitor to make good, out of his own pocket, costs incurred by a client through the solicitor's negligence. Normally, however, matters of discipline within the profession are controlled by a statutory committee of the Incorporated Law Society. This committee can investigate allegations against any solicitor and, in a proper case, refer the matter to the President of the High Court (or another High Court judge nominated by him), who can deal with it, either by removing the offender's name from the roll of solicitors, or otherwise. The power to restore a name to the roll is also vested in the High Court.

It is difficult in a work of such short compass to describe in any detail the duties of a solicitor. In earlier times the work of the solicitor and the work of the barrister were more clearly differentiated than they are today. The solicitor was the practical man of business who carried out the practical work for the client in ordinary commercial matters, in probate, in the making of wills, and in preparing cases for litigation. He also acted as an advocate in the County Court and at Petty Sessions. Now, it can be said, the scope of a solicitor's business has widened enormously. Many new branches of practice have developed in which solicitors have to be as expert as members of the Bar. Questions of taxation law tend to be dealt with more and more by solicitors, and it is only in cases of real difficulty that the competent solicitor will have recourse to counsel. Again, many solicitors today carry through transactions in connection with the promotion of companies and their organisation and management which used formerly to fall within the purview of the Bar. On the other hand, solicitors have tended to do less advocacy, and the right of audience in the High Court conferred on them by the Courts Act 1971 is little exercised except for formal matters.

The Barrister

Barristers are known collectively as 'the Bar' and also collectively (or individually) as 'counsel'. In England, this branch of the legal profession probably first developed with the growth of the voluntary societies called the Inns of Court. These bodies were in reality legal universities, governed by senior members of the profession of the Bar, called Benchers. One of their functions was to make provision for the legal education of students, and there was a comprehensive system of 'readings', mock trials, and courses of instruction. At the end of this, the student was 'called to the Bar' by his Inn, and the judges were prepared to accept the verdict of an Inn of Court on the fitness of a candidate to plead before them as a qualified barrister. Disciplinary control over the barrister was exercised by the Benchers of his Inn of Court, subject to a right of appeal (rarely used) to the judges.

In England (but not in Ireland) there also developed another rank of barrister, the Serjeant-at-Law. These were drawn from the more successful members of the Bar and were admitted to the order of Serjeants by the Lord Chancellor. They maintained their own Inn of Court, the judges were drawn exclusively from their number, and they had an exclusive right of audience in the Court of Common Pleas. In the nineteenth century the order fell into disuse.

In the eighteenth century there also developed another rank or grade of barrister, called a 'King's Counsel.' At first, King's Counsel were appointed for the work of the Crown, but by the beginning of the nineteenth century it became a regular practice for successful practitioners at the Bar to apply for the appointment. Becoming a Queen's Counsel is known as 'taking silk', because the gown then worn is of silk. There were (and are) no special qualifications in England for becoming a Queen's Counsel, other than professional eminence. The appointment is made by the Lord Chancellor, and the successful applicant is issued with a patent of precedence. Taking silk has now got nothing to do with Crown work; the old rule was that a Queen's Counsel could not appear against the Crown without leave, but since 1920 this can now be done.

In Ireland, the fact that for many centuries the common law remained the exclusive perquisite of the Anglo-Norman settlers and their descendants meant, in effect, that those persons aspiring to practise the law must necessarily be of that race. In the absence of any facilities for local training, it seems to have become the custom for potential lawyers to travel to London and to attach themselves to one of the Inns of Court there. This resulted in unfortunate repercussions, and whether it was due to the difference in national temperament or to other factors, Irishmen were far from welcome in these centres of legal learning. It is possible, indeed, that the object in refusing to admit Irishmen to the London Inns was to provide an excuse for exercising judicial preferment in favour of Englishmen, on the ground that no natives were qualified.

One result of this hostility was that, in 1541, the judges and law officers of Ireland presented a memorial to the English Privy Council, in which they set out their grievances in the matter of legal education and prayed that they should be permitted to take a lease of certain premises in Dublin for the purpose of accommodating a legal society already in existence which the petitioners termed 'the King's Inn.' This memorial was accepted and the lease was duly made. At the same time, a statue was passed providing, in effect, that no person was to be admitted to practice at the Bar in Ireland unless he had kept more than one year's law terms at a London Inn. This regulation was greatly resented, but it remained in force until 1885.

King's Inns, however, did not assume any teaching functions with regard to students for the Bar, such as were carried out in the London Inns, and this situation continued right down to the middle of the nineteenth century. Aspirants for call to the Bar were expected to keep a certain number of terms by dining at the Inns, to pay certain fees, and thereupon they were admitted to the degree of barrister-at-law. Admission to practice in the courts lay with the Lord Chancellor, who called the candidate to the Bar in open court.

In 1839, an organisation under the name of The Dublin Law Institute was set up for the purpose of affording legal education for both branches of the profession, and at first, it received financial assistance from King's Inns. This arrangement was a short-lived one, however, and a withdrawal of the grant by the Benchers led to the demise of the Institute. The report of a Select Committee on Legal Education, which appeared in 1846, gave fresh stimulus to the demand for systematic training facilities for the Bar, and in 1850 King's Inns set up a scheme of education for students reading for the Bar which was to be carried out in conjunction with the professors of Trinity College, Dublin.

Today, all candidates for call to the Bar are required to become students of King's Inns, which provides courses of lectures conducted by part-time professors appointed by it, and they are also required to pass examinations in the theory and practice of the law. The full period of study is four years, but this may be shortened in the case of persons who possess a degree in arts, science or law from one of a number of Irish universities. In addition, it is necessary for the Bar student to obtain credit for attendance at certain law courses at Trinity College Dublin, University College Dublin, or University College Cork. Having passed the final examination, eaten the prescribed number of dinners and passed an Irish test, the student is duly called to the Bar. At this stage, the tyro, in theory at any rate, is fitted to appear in any court in the state, but, in practice, it is usual (but not compulsory) in the first year to 'devil', that is, become a pupil of a practising member of the junior Bar (the 'master') to acquire the necessary technical expertise. On the other hand, many candidates for call to the Bar do not intend to practise, but wish to obtain a relatively cheap and speedy professional qualification which will enable them to obtain employment in industry, in the civil service, or in the local government service.

At the Bar, the Attorney General is the head of the profession. Since the new courts were established in 1924, barristers are no longer admitted to the rank of King's or Queen's Counsel; a new rank, identical in function with the old, and called 'senior counsel', was devised. Applications to take silk are addressed to the Chief Justice but, it seems, the power to issue patents for call to the inner bar is vested in the government. Senior counsel take precedence in order of call within the Bar, as do junior counsel *inter se*. Discipline over the profession is still vested in the Benchers of King's Inns, but there is also a democratically elected body, the General Council of the Bar, composed partly of seniors and partly of juniors, elected by all the practising barristers. This body assists in disciplinary matters and superintends the general interests of the profession.

Training for the Legal Profession

Apart from the professional education provided for solicitors and barristers by their respective bodies, courses in law are conducted at the two universities in the Republic. The fact that both the professional bodies grant certain exemptions to students who are attending a university or who possess a degree might serve to indicate that these bodies give tacit recognition that the universities alone are competent to impart a scientific training in law. Since this exemption is granted for degrees in arts as well as law, however, there is little force in the argument; and a man may still become a solicitor in the Republic of Ireland without having read law (or anything else) at a university. The concessions by King's Inns and the Incorporated Law Society do, nevertheless, make it clear that they recognise the theoretical advisability of a university training.

A university degree in law, as such, confers no right on the holder to practise law, and although the nature of a university training is such that its law teaching may be of a theoretical nature, the fact that there exist in the Republic four separate university schools of law, each one independent of the other, and none of them satisfactorily coordinated with the professional bodies, is in itself a condemnation of the whole system. The part the universities ought properly to play in professional legal education is a matter for debate, but be that as it may, the present position cannot be correct. The universities attempt to fulfil a dual role; in part they teach law and grant degrees in it as an academic exercise, and, in addition, they act as law schools for the professional bodies. As a result, they have fallen between two stools, for though they have tried to subordinate the latter role to the former, to compel Bar students and solicitors' apprentices to attend the normal degree courses is in effect to constrict the nature and scope of these academic courses within a narrow and professional straitjacket.

From time to time the suggestion is put forward that a possible solution to the problems of the legal profession in the Republic of Ireland would be to fuse the two branches of the profession, but, it is thought, this does not provide an answer to the most important questions. It is noteworthy that even in those common law countries which have effected a compulsory fusion of this type, or where the division has never existed, the *de facto* separation into the advocate and the office-lawyer is preserved. It is probably true to say that, in the superior courts, cases are better presented in the interests of the clients if the function of putting the case before the court is separated from that of preparing it for hearing. Moreover, the employment of both solicitors and barristers in the preparation and presentation of a case does not involve the client in more expense than he would incur if the same person, or firm, were to perform both functions.

It is in the field of legal training, however, that the greatest shortcomings are manifest. In the practice of the law today, a sound theoretical training in law is becoming more and more important for both the solicitor and the barrister, and it is generally admitted that such training is best provided in the universities. At the moment, there is a great deal of overlapping between the professional training of each branch, and much of this could be eliminated by providing a combined course, up to university degree level, for both potential solicitors and potential barristers. Thereafter, having passed a qualifying examination, each could proceed to his own professional training and final examination, and at some appropriate moment each student would have to decide whether he wanted to be a solicitor or a barrister.

At the same time, all law students should be encouraged to proceed to a university degree in law, and the possession of such a degree would exempt the holder from the qualifying examination at the end of the combined course, or university courses might be accepted as a substitute for such course. So far as can be ascertained, there is no other profession which expresses any hesitation concerning the teaching of its subject at a university. It is only the professional lawyers who seem to be doubtful whether their subject can properly be taught within academic walls.

All this would entail the shortening of the period of apprenticeship served by potential solicitors, but a certain amount of dovetailing might be achieved by severing the period into two or more shorter terms. In addition, it is thought, the appointment of a director of studies by each of the professional bodies, to ensure that each student's time was occupied to the best advantage, would be of considerable assistance. Apprentices to solicitors should be properly remunerated for their work, and the system of premiums, under which the apprentice pays his master a fee for his instruction, should be abolished. Compulsory pupillage for the newly-called barrister might also be prescribed, and it could be argued that a short period in a solicitor's office would enable him to see how the other branch of the profession does its work. It should be made easier for a barrister to become a solicitor, and vice versa, and in that event it is important that the barrister should be properly qualified to do solicitors' work and the solicitor properly qualified to do barristers' work, after the change had taken place.

Finally, for both professions, there should be some form of pre-entry selection tests, designed to assess the candidate's suitability, on intellectual and moral grounds, for admission to the practice of the law. Such a test has been in force in the United States for about thirty years, though it was not introduced without a long and bitter struggle. The opponents of the test apparently based their arguments on the undeclared major premise that all men have the inherent right to practise law. They contended that the practice of the law must not become the privilege of the well-to-do; and that educational requirements create economic barriers for worthy but indigent students. Those favouring admission tests sought to impress the view that the privilege of practising law is a matter of public concern; that the lawyer is the spokesman for others; that, in representing others, their property, their liberty, and, indeed, their lives may depend on the skill with which he works; and that it follows that the privilege to practise law should be given only to persons of proved learning, integrity and competence.

The introduction of a test in order to determine intellectual and moral fitness for entry into the legal profession would at least help to exclude those who were unlikely to make successful lawyers, and it would also give guidance to those who were in doubt as to the branch of the profession for which they were best suited. The intricate and costly machinery of justice is provided by the people of the country as a whole, and the real need is to awaken public opinion to the necessity of producing a generation of lawyers who are properly qualified for their chosen profession, and who will not have to learn it at the expense of their clients' property or liberty.

CHAPTER X

THE FINANCES OF THE LAW

The Finances of the Courts of Justice

In the early days of the common law, the Royal Courts were expected to be financially self-supporting. The judges and the court officials remunerated themselves from the fees paid by the litigants. In modern times, however, though some part of the cost of litigation is thrown on those who resort to them, nevertheless the burden of supporting the courts falls on public funds.

The administration of the criminal law, in particular, is a public charge. The judges are, of course, paid officials of the state, but also the cost of conducting prosecutions is a charge on the finances of the country as a whole. In the civil courts, on the other hand, the litigant has to make a substantial contribution towards the cost of his action. He has to pay the appropriate fees; he has to bear the expense of collecting evidence and bringing his witnesses to court; and he has to pay the fees of his solicitor and counsel. The general principle adopted in modern times has been that while the state pays the judicial salaries, the courts should, so far as is possible, be self-supporting. In other words, the wages and pensions of the court officials, and the provision and maintenance of buildings and equipment, should be capable of being recouped out of the court fees paid by the litigants. This principle applies in the inferior tribunals as well as in the High Court.

Costs

The expression 'costs' is usually employed to describe all those expenses of litigation which one party has to pay to the other. In ordinary litigation, the machinery of payment works in the following way. The client authorises his solicitor to bring, or defend, the proceedings, and the normal result is that the winner is awarded his costs. Historically, the situation is that in actions at common law, the right to be paid costs depends entirely on statute, and they follow the event, i.e., the winner is paid them automatically. In the Court of Chancery, on the other hand, the Chancellor always regarded the award of costs as being a matter for his discretion, and he would deprive a successful suitor of them, if he thought he had acted inequitably.

Today, there are two types of costs to be considered. Any party to an action, whether he has won or not, must pay his own solicitor all the solicitor's proper charges and disbursements for conducting the litigation in accordance with the client's express or implied instructions. These are called 'solicitor and client costs.' On the other hand, the costs that must be paid by the loser to the winner of an action are calculated on a different basis, the idea being that the loser must pay only such costs and expenses as have been "necessarily or properly incurred" for the conduct of the case. In practice, each side will have spent more than was strictly necessary, because they will have thought it prudent to be prepared for any eventuality in the course of the trial.

In order to arrive at the sum the loser must pay, the winner's solicitor sends a bill of costs to the loser's solicitor. If it is agreed, it is paid forthwith, but if the latter disputes it, then the bill is submitted to 'taxation.' This is a species of machinery whereby an official called the Taxing Master provides a hearing at which the loser's solicitor may object to the disputed items. Each disputed item is discussed, and allowed or disallowed by the master. In exercising his discretion, the master has before him all the relevant papers in the case so that he may judge the difficulty and importance of the point involved, and there is an appeal to a judge of the High Court against his decision. In the Circuit Court, this function is performed by the County Registrar.

The process of taxation of costs ensures that a party who has conducted his action along extravagant lines cannot make the loser pay for that extravagance. When the taxation is completed, the sum allowed is called 'party and party costs.' If an action is settled before the hearing, a sum is sometimes agreed for party and party costs, and on occasions for solicitor and client costs also, but most settlements contain a provision that the costs are to be taxed in default of agreement. It is also possible for a client who considers that his own solicitor and client bill of costs is too high to have it taxed. This involves a consideration of the nature of the instructions given by the client to the solicitor, for the point is not the figure at which the work could have been done, but whether the solicitor has charged properly for the work he was instructed to do. The actual taxation of the bill itself also involves costs, and the general rule is that if less than one-sixth of the bill is disallowed, the costs of the taxation are borne by the party challenging the bill, while if the bill is reduced by more than one-sixth, the party claiming on the bill must pay the costs.

At this stage, it must be made clear that the costs which a solicitor may lawfully charge are to a large extent regulated by statute. For the purpose of estimating costs, a solicitor's work is divided into 'contentious' and 'non-contentious' business. Contentious work is that carried on in connection with court proceedings, and the charges here are regulated by the Rules of Court. For non-contentious work, such as conveyancing, there is also a scale of charges based on the purchase price of the property.

When a solicitor prepares a bill of costs for submission to his own client or to the other party to an action, the bill is made up of two items, 'disbursements' and 'profit costs.' Disbursements are the amounts paid by the solicitor on behalf of his client, such as court fees, stamp duties, counsel's fees, witnesses' expenses, and so on. Profit costs are the solicitor's charges for his own work, though before he arrives at his net profit costs he must set off against the gross amount chargeable the cost of his offices, staff salaries, and kindred items. The preparation of such a bill of costs is a highly complicated business, for each item must be set out separately, with its appropriate charge. Normally, it would be fair to state that with respect to profit costs, about 70 per cent. goes in the expense of running an office, leaving 30 per cent. as net costs for the solicitor.

By way of contrast, the fees of members of the Bar are not regulated in any way by any statutory authority, for while the profession itself does prescribe minimum fees, this is designed to protect the Bar itself, and not the public. Normally, a member of the Bar, in contentious business, will charge such a fee as he feels his services are worth, with the addition that where both senior and junior counsel are engaged (and, in most cases, it is contrary to the etiquette of the Bar for a senior to appear without a junior), the fee payable to the junior will be two-thirds of that of a senior's fee. Apart from certain prescribed fees charged by counsel in connection with the settling of the form of proceedings, and with certain inter-locutory applications to the court, the major part of the fee paid to counsel is the 'fee on brief'—the lump sum payable to him for conducting the case in court. This may or may not be accompanied by a series of 'refresher' fees, payable in the event of the case lasting more than a specified time. In addition, a fee will be paid to counsel for attending a consultation with the client.

So far as the payment of counsel's fees is concerned, the position is that counsel is employed by the solicitor, and not by the client, and if the solicitor agrees to pay a certain fee to counsel, he is morally bound to do so, notwithstanding that it is later disallowed on taxation against his client. Unlike the English practice, it is not customary in the Republic of Ireland to find two junior counsel engaged in a case, though it is perhaps more usual than not to find two senior counsel and one junior so engaged. The reason for this is difficult to justify, unless it reflects the disproportionately large number of senior counsel in practice, a state of affairs which can probably be attributed to the desire to earn substantially higher fees, coupled with the ease with which the rank can be attained.

The fact that the costs are always, or nearly always, payable by the loser can have some curious effects on litigation. Thus X may claim £1,000 damages from Y, and Y may think that £1,000 is a fair estimate of his liability. He may offer £900 in settlement, which X will be advised to accept, for it is better to get £900 in a settlement than to get a judgment for £1,000 and have to pay out, say, £150 over and above what he can recover in costs from Y. It is extremely difficult to say what, in practice, represents the actual cost of litigation, for a solicitor will usually conduct a suit in accordance with what his client is willing and able to spend. Solicitors' charges are not excessive for the amount of work involved, and it is really impossible to do anything about the cost of litigation as a whole so long as persons are permitted to spend what they like in going to law. It is arguable that some scheme might be introduced whereby persons were limited in the amount they could spend on litigation, but it seems that that day is still far away.

Legal Aid

Under the adversary system, the proper presentation of cases on behalf of parties is an essential pre-condition of the effective administration of justice. This poses problems where people are without means to employ lawyers to advise them and present their case to best advantage in court. Both branches of the legal profession in Ireland have always regarded it as a duty to advise and assist impecunious persons without charge. In addition, various social, charitable and religious bodies have on occasion obtained the free services of solicitors and, where necessary, counsel to assist poor persons. The Criminal Justice (Legal Aid) Act 1962 made provision for grants out of public funds to enable accused persons without means to employ solicitors and counsel to defend them. It is limited to cases of murder or where the serious nature of the offence or other exceptional circumstances render it necessary to give legal aid in the interests of justice. The scheme has inevitably encountered teething problems. In December 1974, the solicitors withdrew from it in protest against delays by the Department of Justice in processing their claim for improved conditions and fees. Previously, in 1970, the Bar, had, for a time, declined to participate on account of the inadequacy of the fees, and reverted to the practice of making their services available to impecunious clients free of charge. They have argued that the interests of justice require parity of fees for prosecution and defence counsel. The hope has also been expressed that legal aid should be made available for a broader range of crimes.

In civil cases, there is no provision for legal aid out of public funds. The bulk of civil actions brought by impecunious persons are claims for damages for injuries sustained in road traffic or industrial accidents. If a solicitor is instructed by an impecunious client and he is satisfied that there is a reasonable chance of success, he may not be prevented from bringing his action because of lack of funds on the part of his client, but may undertake to pay out of his own pocket any necessary expenses, such as fees to doctors, engineers and other witnesses, and to be responsible for counsel's fees. In such a case the solicitor is taking a chance on the outcome. If the action is successful, costs will be awarded against the defendant on a 'party and party' basis, and any 'solicitor and client' items will be recoverable out of the damages awarded to the client. The solicitor will thus be able to recover his disbursements and his profit costs. If the action fails, then the solicitor will be at the loss of any out-of-pocket expenses and he will not receive any profit costs. It is, of course, unprofessional for a solicitor to take on such a case on the understanding that if the action is successful the client will pay a larger sum in costs than would be allowed on taxation.

Such a speculative action is open to a number of objections. In the first place, it is unjust that the possibility of a litigant commencing proceedings should depend on the fortuitous circumstances of finding a solicitor who will take on his case. Secondly, it is wrong in principle that the remuneration of a solicitor should depend on the chance of success in the action. Thirdly, litigants of this type may find themselves intimidated into settling an action in which they have a good ground for obtaining damages. Lastly, the increasing cost of office administration and the rise in professional charges will render it inevitable that this type of action will become more and more rare.

Since the introduction of apportionment of damages in road traffic and industrial accident cases according to the relative degree of fault of those involved, plaintiffs seldom fail to obtain some damages. This means that there are usually funds out of which legal fees can be paid. However, in other litigation, notably constitutional and matrimonial cases, a client may fail completely, leaving no funds out of which fees can be paid. The increase of these latter categories of litigation, as well as the objections noted to speculative actions, has pinpointed the necessity for legal aid in civil cases. In the first half of 1974, the government set up a committee under the chairmanship of the former Mr Justice Pringle to consider the matter.

In England a system of legal aid and advice for impecunious litigants has been in force since 1949. It is now regulated by the Legal Aid Act 1974. This scheme is not 'free legal aid' in the sense of being absolutely free, and all who are able to do so are required to make a contribution. The solicitors' professional body, the Law Society, administers the scheme through local committees. These committees decide if a litigant has an arguable case and also the contribution a person of his means should make to his costs. Solicitors and barristers willing to act for persons receiving legal aid enter their names on a panel from which applicants make their own choice. If, in addition to the costs (if any) recovered on behalf of an assisted person, the whole of the contribution is not required by the Law Society to pay the solicitor and counsel, then the balance is repaid to him. In addition to providing assistance in proceedings in court, the English legislation introduced a system of legal advice in non-contentious matters for those unable to pay for it. There is also provision for preliminary legal aid in order to investigate a possible claim or defence prior to the granting of legal aid in connection with bringing or defending proceedings.

The provision of legal aid does not remove all imperfections in the administration of justice arising from the necessity to pay legal costs. Persons of moderate means who are not covered by such a scheme may be deterred from embarking on litigation by the prospect of the costs that they may have to meet if they lose. With the emergence of civil legal aid, litigation could well become a luxury reserved for the very rich and the very poor unless some means is found of providing a subvention for those of moderate means. There is no reason why the sifting process applied in deciding whether an impecunious person has a good enough case to merit legal aid should not also be applied to those of moderate means who should, perhaps, be protected against outsize costs.

FURTHER READING

Ball, F. Elrington *The Judges in Ireland 1221-1921*, 2 volumes (London: John Murray, 1926).

Ball, John Thomas *Historical Review of the Legislative Systems Operative in Ireland 1172-1800* (London: Longman Green, 2nd ed. 1889).

Bartholomew, Paul C. *The Irish Judiciary* (Dublin: Institute of Public Administration, 1971).

Beth, Loren P. *The Development of Judicial Review in Ireland 1937-1966* (Dublin: Institute of Public Administration, 1967).

Delany, V. T. H. "The Constitution of Ireland: Its Origins and Development", *University of Toronto Law Journal*, 12 (1957-58), 1-26.

"The History of Legal Education in Ireland", *Journal of Legal Education*, 12 (1960), 396-406.

Donaldson, Alfred Gaston *Some Comparative Aspects of Irish Law* (Cambridge: Cambridge University Press, 1957).

Grogan, Vincent *Administrative Tribunals in the Public Service* (Dublin: Institute of Public Administration, 1961).

"The Constitution and Natural Law", *Christus Rex*, 8 (1954), 201-18.

"Irish Constitutional Development", *Studies*, 40 (1951), 385-98.

Hand, G. J. *English Law in Ireland 1290-1324* (Cambridge: Cambridge University Press, 1967).

Hanna, H. and Pringle, A. D. *The Statute Law of the Irish Free State 1922-1928* (Dublin: Thom, 1929).

Johnston, W. J. "The First Adventure of the Common Law", *Law Quarterly Review*, 36 (1920), 9-30.

Kaim-Caudle, P. R. "Productivity, Income and Standards of Solicitors in the Irish Republic", *The Irish Jurist* (new series) V (1970), 40.

Keane, Ronan "The Future of the Irish Bar", *Studies,* 54 (1965).

Kelly, John M. *Fundamental Rights in the Irish Law and Constitution* (Dublin: Figgis, 1961; 2nd ed. 1967).

Knight, Michael "The Irish Court of Criminal Appeal", *The Irish Jurist* (new series) IV (1969) 91, 247.

Kohn, Leo *The Constitution of the Irish Free State* (London: Allen and Unwin, 1932).

MacDermott, Lord "Law and Practice in Northern Ireland", *Northern Ireland Legal Quarterly,* 10 (1952-54), 47-77.

"The Supreme Court of Northern Ireland—Two Unusual Jurisdictions", *Journal of the Society of Public Teachers of Law* (new series) 2 (1954), 201-13.

MacNeill, J. G. S. *Studies in the Constitution of the Irish Free State* (Dublin and Cork: Talbot Press, 1925).

McWhinney, Edward *Judicial Review* (Toronto: University of Toronto Press, 4th ed. 1969).

Manseragh, Nicholas *The Irish Free State: Its Government and Politics* (London: Allen and Unwin, 1934).

Newark, F. H. *Notes on Irish Legal History* (Belfast: Boyd, 1960).

O'Flanagan, J. R. *Lives of the Lord Chancellors of Ireland,* 2 volumes (London: Longman Green, 1810).

O'Sullivan, Donal *The Irish Free State and Its Senate* (London: Faber and Faber, 1940).

Plunkett, Eric A. "Solicitors in the Republic: A Reply to the Professors", *The Irish Jurist* (new series) VI (1971), 18.

Quekett, Sir Arthur S. *The Constitution of Northern Ireland,* 3 volumes (Belfast: HMSO, 1928, 1933, 1946).

Sheridan, L. A. "Irish Private Law and the English Lawyer", *International and Comparative Law Quarterly,* 1 (1952), 196-212.

"Northern Ireland" in George W. Keeton and Dennis Lloyd (eds) *The United Kingdom: The Development of its Laws and Constitutions* (London: Stevens, 1955).

Reports of the Committee on Court Practice and Procedure (Dublin: Stationery Office, 1964-74).

INDEX

Anglo-Irish Treaty (1921), 33, 34, 36

Appeals
  before 1921, 20-22, 29-30
  from 1924, 40-42
  case stated, 51, 53, 68, 69, 70
  criminal, 49-53, 68, 70
  civil, 63-65, 68, 69, 70
  to European Courts, 65

Assistant Barrister, 75, 81

Assize, Commissions of, 14, 24-26, 27, 29, 41, 43, 44, 78

Attorney General, 27, 41, 44, 45, 49, 52, 73, 74, 76, 82, 83, 89
  see also Director of Public Prosecutions

Bar, The, *see* Barristers

Barristers, 36, 87-92, 95-96

Brehon law, 16

Central Criminal Court, 40, 47, 48, 49, 51

Certiorari, writ of, 30, 50

Chancellor, *see* Lord Chancellor, Lord Chancellor of Ireland

Chief Justice, 51, 70, 72, 73, 75, 81

Chief Justice of Irish Free State, 40, 41, 75

Children's Court, The, 48

Circuit Court of Justice, 40, 47-53, 55, 61, 66-69, 70, 79, 82

Circuits, 24, 79

Civil bill, 28-29, 67-68

Clerk of the Crown, 81

Clerk of the Peace, 81

Commission for the City of Dublin, 26, 40, 49

Commission of goal delivery, 14, 22, 24

Commission of oyer and terminer, 14, 22, 24

Commission of the Peace, 30-31

Committee on Court Practice and Procedure, Reports of, 47, 48, 52, 53, 62, 64, 67, 70

Common Law, 2, 9-11, 23, 58-59
  introduction to Ireland, 13, 15-18

Constitution of Ireland, 7, 8, 12, 41, 46, 47, 52, 63-66, 73, 75, 83

Constitution of the Irish Free State (1922), 7, 8, 33-34, 71-72

Cork Local Admiralty Court, 69

Cork Local Bankruptcy Court, 69

Costs, legal, 93-99

County Courts, 28-30, 36, 39, 40, 86

County Registrar, 82, 94

Court for the Relief of Insolvent Debtors, 22

Court of Appeal (England), 6

Court of Appeal (Ireland), 8, 23

Court of Appeal in Chancery, 21, 22

Court of Bankruptcy and Insolvency, 22, 23

Court of Chancery (England), 10-11, 15, 19, 21, 23, 58, 79, 94

Court of Chancery (Ireland), 20-23, 79

Court of Common Pleas (England), 14-15, 58, 84, 87

Court of Common Pleas (Ireland), 17, 19-23, 78, 79

Court of Criminal Appeal, 41, 42, 51-52, 78

Court of Crown Cases Reserved, 22

Court of Exchequer (England), 14, 21, 23, 58, 79

Court of Exchequer (Ireland), 17, 19-21, 78, 79

Court of Exchequer Chamber (Ireland), 21

Court of the High Court Circuit (1924-1926), 41

Court of the Irish Land Commission, 24

Court of Justice of the European Communities, 65

Court of King's (or Queen's) Bench (England), 15, 20, 21, 58, 84

Court of King's (or Queen's) Bench (Ireland), 17, 23, 31, 78, 79

Court of Matrimonial Causes and Matters, 22, 23

Court of Prerogative and Faculties, 19, 21, 22

Court of Probate, 22, 23

Court of the High Court Circuit, 41

Court of the Irish Land Commission, 24

Courts of Dáil Éireann (1919-1921), 35-37, 38

Courts of local jurisdiction, 26-31

Crown Solicitors, 44

Curia Regis, 9, 13, 14, 17

Dáil Courts *see* Courts of Dáil Éireann

Dáil Éireann, 33, 34

Director of Public Prosecutions, 45, 47, 48, 49

District Court, 40, 45, 46-48, 49, 50, 54, 66, 69-70, 79, 82 *see also* Courts of Dáil Éireann

District Justices, 38-39, 40, 44, 45, 50, 54, 73, 76

Dublin Law Institute, The, 88

Education, legal, 89-92

Equity, 9-11, 17, 23

European Commission of Human Rights, 65

European Convention on Human Rights, 65

Governor-General of the Irish Free State, 38

Grand Jury, 27, 44-45

Habeas Corpus, 53

High Court, 39-42, 49, 50-51, 57-58, 61, 62, 64, 68, 79, 81, 86

High Court (continued)
Master of, 21, 60, 63, 81
President of, 40, 41, 75,
81, 86
see also Central Criminal
Court
High Court of Admiralty,
19-20, 21, 22, 23
High Court of Appeal for
Ireland (1921-1922), 32, 38
High Court of Justice
(1877-1924), 23, 24, 30, 38
House of Lords, 6, 8, 17, 20,
21, 32
House of Lords (Kingdom of
Ireland), 20

Incorporated Law Society of
Ireland, 36, 85, 86, 90
Incumbered Estates Court,
The, 21
Indictable offences, 46-49,
52-55
Indictment, bill of, 27, 44
Inferior Courts see under
individual courts
Inns of Court, 84, 87
Irish Court of King's Bench,
17, 19, 20, 23
Irish Reports, The, 5-6

Judges
appointment of, 73-74,
76-77
retirement of, 74, 76
salaries of, 75-76
tenure of, 71, 73-75
Judgments, Enforcement of,
63
Jurisdiction
appellate see Appeals
of District Court, 40, 46-48,
69-70
of Circuit Court, 40, 48,
66-69
of High Court, 40, 49, 66
of Supreme Court, 40-41
summary, 43
Jury, trial by, Chapter 6
passim, 61-62
Justices of the Peace, 26-28,
30, 38, 40, 43
Justiciar, 15, 17

King's Advocate, 82
King's Counsel, 87
King's Inns, Honourable
Society of, 77, 85, 88, 90

Landed Estates Court, 21, 23
Law Club, 85
Law Reports, The, 5, 6, 7, 11,
12
Law Society of Ireland, 85
Legal aid, 97-99
Legal training, 89-92
Legislation, a source of law,
3, 4, 17-18
Lord Chancellor, 9-10, 19,
58, 74, 87, 94
see also Court of Chancery
Lord Chancellor of Ireland,
21-23, 32, 40-41, 74
Lord Chief Justice of Ireland,
19, 23
Lord Chief Justice of the
Common Pleas, 19, 23
Lord Chief Justice of
Northern Ireland, 32
Lord Chief Justice of
Southern Ireland, 32
Lord Lieutenant of Ireland,
28, 81
Lord Treasurer, 9, 14, 21

Mandamus, writ of, 30, 50
Master in Chancery, 79
Master of the High Court, *see*
  High Court, Master of
Minister for Justice, 73, 79

Obiter dicta, 7
Office of Wards of Court, 81
Officers of the courts, 79-83
Oireachtas, *see* Parliament

Parliament
  see also Dáil Éireann
  of England, 17
  of the Kingdom of Ireland,
  4, 17, 18
  of the United Kingdom, 4
  of Southern Ireland, 34
  the Oireachtas, 4, 42
Peace Commissioners, 40, 54
Petty Sessions, courts of, 27,
  36, 38, 40, 82, 86
Pleadings, 58-60, 68
Precedent, doctrine of, 4-9, 11
  foreign, 11, 12
Prerogative writs, 30, 50, 53
President of the High Court,
  40, 41, 49, 75, 81, 86
Prime Serjeant, 82
Privy Council of Ireland, 16,
  21, 22
Procedure
  civil cases, 57-58, 60-63,
  67, 68, 70
  criminal cases, 44, 54-55
Prohibition, writ of, 30, 50

Quarter Sessions, courts of,
  26-27, 29, 39, 43, 44

Ratio decidendi, 6-7
Recorder's Court, 29
Resident Magistrates, 28, 38,
  44, 75
Roman Law, 2, 11, 36

Royal Irish Constabulary, 28
Rules of Court, 57-60, 95

Select Committee on Legal
  Education, 88
Senior Counsel, 87
Serjeant-at-Law, 82, 87
Sittings, court, 77-79
Society of Attorneys and
  Solicitors of Ireland, 85
Solicitor General, 82
Solicitors, 84-86, 90-92, 94,
  95, 96
  crown, 44
  state, 44
Special Criminal Courts, 49
Summary offences, 27, 43, 46,
  54
Summons, 54
  summary, 60
  plenary, 60, 61
Superior Courts, *see under*
  individual courts
Supreme Court, 39, 40-41, 42,
  52-53, 57, 63-65, 68, 69,
  78, 79
  Rules Committee, 57
Supreme Court of Judicature
  in Ireland (1877-1921), 23,
  33, 39, 80
Supreme Court of Judicature
  in Southern Ireland
  (1921-1924), 32-33, 36, 37,
  75

Taxing Master, 94
Textbooks, legal, source of
  law, 11, 12
Terms, legal, 77, 78
Treaty of Rome (1955), 65

Writs, 9, 58-60

Year Books, 5